CRACK THE C INTERVIEW

AF647622

Dr. Sachin Kadam

B. Tech. Computer, MCA, PGDES, Ph.D.,
Professor in Computer Application,
Institute of Management & Entrepreneurship Development,
Bharati Vidyapeeth University, Pune.
Mob. No.: 9881372633.

Prof. Hanumant Namdeo Renushe

MCA, M.Phil., Ph.D.,
Assistant Professor, Bharati Vidyapeeth Deemed University,
Yashwantrao Mohite Institute of Management, Karad.

HPH

Himalaya Publishing House

MUMBAI • NEW DELHI • NAGPUR • BENGALURU • HYDERABAD • CHENNAI • PUNE • LUCKNOW • AHMEDABAD • ERNAKULAM • BHUBANESWAR • INDORE • KOLKATA • GUWAHATI

First Edition : 2012

Published by : Mrs. Meena Pandey for **Himalaya Publishing House Pvt. Ltd.,**
"Ramdoot", Dr. Bhalerao Marg, Girgaon, **Mumbai - 400 004.**
Phone: 022-23860170/23863863, Fax: 022-23877178
E-mail: himpub@vsnl.com; Website: www.himpub.com

Branch Offices :

New Delhi : "Pooja Apartments", 4-B, Murari Lal Street, Ansari Road, Darya Ganj, New Delhi - 110 002. Phone: 011-23270392, 23278631; Fax: 011-23256286

Nagpur : Kundanlal Chandak Industrial Estate, Ghat Road, Nagpur - 440 018. Phone: 0712-2738731, 3296733; Telefax: 0712-2721215

Bengaluru : No. 16/1 (Old 12/1), 1st Floor, Next to Hotel Highlands, Madhava Nagar, Race Course Road, Bengaluru - 560 001. Phone: 080-32919385; Telefax: 080-22286611

Hyderabad : No. 3-4-184, Lingampally, Besides Raghavendra Swamy Matham, Kachiguda, Hyderabad - 500 027. Phone: 040-27560041, 27550139; Mobile: 09390905282

Chennai : No. 8/2, Madley 2nd Street, Ground Floor, T. Nagar, Chennai - 600 017. Phone: 044-28144004/28144005; Mobile: 09345345051

Pune : First Floor, "Laksha" Apartment, No. 527, Mehunpura, Shaniwarpeth (Near Prabhat Theatre), Pune - 411 030. Phone: 020-24496323/24496333; Mobile: 09370579333

Lucknow : House No 731, Shekhupura Colony, Near B.D. Convent School, Aliganj, Lucknow - 226 022. Mobile: 09307501549

Ahmedabad : 114, "SHAIL", 1st Floor, Opp. Madhu Sudan House, C.G. Road, Navrang Pura, Ahmedabad - 380 009. Phone: 079-26560126; Mobile: 09377088847

Ernakulam : 39/176 (New No: 60/251) 1st Floor, Karikkamuri Road, Ernakulam, Kochi - 682011, Phone: 0484-2378012, 2378016; Mobile: 09344199799

Bhubaneswar : 5 Station Square, Bhubaneswar - 751 001 (Odisha). Phone: 0674-2532129, Mobile: 09338746007

Indore : Kesardeep Avenue Extension, 73, Narayan Bagh, Flat No. 302, IIIrd Floor, Near Humpty Dumpty School, Indore - 452 007 (M.P.). Mobile: 09301386468

Kolkata : 108/4, Beliaghata Main Road, Near ID Hospital, Opp. SBI Bank, Kolkata - 700 010, Phone: 033-32449649, Mobile: 09883055590, 07439040301

Guwahati : House No. 15, Behind Pragjyotish College, Near Sharma Printing Press, P.O. Bharalumukh, Guwahati - 781009, (Assam). Mobile: 09883055590, 09883055536

DTP by : HPH, Editorial Office, Bhandup **(Krunali).**

'ted at : M/s. Aditya Offset Process (I) Pvt. Ltd., Hyderabad. On behalf of HPH.

Dedication

To my wife Anita

— Thanks for enriching my life.

....Dr. Sachin Kadam

To my wife Archana and son Raj

— Thanks for being there

....Prof. Hanumant Renushe

Preface

C language is considered to be the most romantic language in computer domain. It allows the programmers to create their own worlds and set their own laws to govern those worlds. Generally, C is encountered as the first computer programming language by many of the programmers. On the outset C appears to be a very modest language with just 32 keywords in its arsenal. The supported programming constructs also appear to be very primitive. But this simplistic approach itself gives C the power to dazzle a programmer with its intricacies. C assumes that the programmers know what they are doing. It does not care to put extra constraints on the programmers to curtail their freedom of expression. This makes C a very powerful language. But' as the saying goes, with power the programmers need to be more responsible towards what they are doing.

This is an unconventional book on C language. This book *"Crack the C Interview"* does not claim to be an exhaustive guide on C programming. The readers of this book is expected to have intermediate knowledge of C language with hands-on experience. This book is designed to help the reader to crack the C interviews. Proficiency in C is one of the measures adopted by the industry for the new recruits. The IT companies follow different approaches to test proficiency of the candidates in C domain. These approaches range from objective tests in C to real-world problem-solving using C. But one characteristic underlines all of these approaches. It is meant to test a candidate's understanding of C language intricacies. This book nails upon the same.

This book tries to elaborate the intricacies of C language from multiple viewpoint; like objective tests, puzzles and FAQs. Also, it deals with the mysteries involving the processing and execution of C programs. Industry expects the C programmers to apply their skill set on multiple platforms. This is also taken care of in the book.

Logically, this book is divided into seven sections. Section-I is a short refresher course on C language. Prior experience with C programming is expected here. This section does not intend to teach the C language. It takes an overview of the C language at an advanced level.

Section-II deals with mostly neglected aspects of C programming; namely processing and execution of a C program. Generally, a C programmer never bothers about the background activities involved in the processing of a C program. The conversion process of C source code file(s) to the final executable file is a fascinating process. A thorough understanding of the same gives the programmers a better understanding of the C language and provides intellectual satisfaction. The execution of the resultant executable is also shrouded in mystery. A thorough understanding of the binary contents of an executable file provides the insight into this. The chapters from this section will unravel these mysteries.

In theory, the understanding of C language is independent of the development tools being used by the programmers. But, in reality, the tools used by the programmers affect the capability and efficiency of the applications written in C. Numerous Integrated Development Environments (IDEs) are also available to enhance the productivity of a C programmer. The awareness of various C programming toolkits and IDEs is essential for a professional C programmer. Section-III will briefly discuss the popular C programming toolkits and IDEs. Its objective is to provide a glimpse of available options to professional C programmers.

C language is available on all the platforms. A platform is a combination of the underlying processor and the operating system. As a programmer one needs to worry only about the operating system factor. The respective toolkit available for that operating system takes care of the underlying processor. The most common operating systems confronted by today's programmers are Windows and Linux. Generally, they confront DOS during their academic tenure. Applying the knowledge of C language on different operating systems requires a programmer to learn appropriate toolkits and IDEs available on those systems. Section-IV briefly discusses C programming under DOS, Windows and Linux environments. It follows a case study-based approach for the sake of brevity.

Converting the theoretical knowledge about C language into a skill-set is a tricky scenario. The professional C programmers needs the proficiency to process a C program in the brain. They have to think as if they are the language processors and visualise the entire processing path. This gives them insight for the C language. Reading and mentally processing a C program helps to develop this skill-set. Section-V gives ample opportunity for the reader for the same. The questions listed down in this section are the representatives of their multiple possible variants. Each listed question is followed by its answer and brief explanation. A reader is suggested to perform mental-processing on the problem first and then compare the answer. Then compare your understanding with the noted explanation. Here the process of mental-processing is more important to develop the professional skill-set of a C programmer.

Section-VI continues on the same theme from previous section. The difference is, purposely explanations and answers are not provided here. Wherever required, depending upon the difficulty level of the problem, suggestive notes are provided to help the readers. The readers can test their understanding of C language by solving the puzzles in this section on their own. In case of any difficulty the reader is encouraged to refer back to the similar problems from previous section to enforce your understanding.

The last section, Section-VII, tests the understanding of C language from objective perspective. It contains ten objective tests. Each test contains 50 questions each. Each question has four options, out of which the reader is supposed to select the correct option(s). The correct answers are provided at the end of the each test. The reader is encouraged to take these tests in competitive spirit. Each test should be ideally timed for 60 minutes. At the end of the test the reader should compare the answers with the ones provided. To bridge the semantic gap in understanding the reader is encouraged to refer back to the Section-V for similar kinds of problems.

We hope that this book will prove to be an important addition to the toolkit of a professional C programmer.

Dr. Sachin Kadam

Prof. Hanumant Renushe

Acknowledgements

I first want to thank my parents for their unconditional love and care for which there is no logic. I really thank Lord Shree Krishna for providing me such considerate guardians on this earth. I want to acknowledge my beautiful wife Anita for her constant love and support. I could not have completed this book without her behind-the scene support, understanding, encouragement and excellent food. A big thanks to my wonderful daughter, Bhondu Niku, without whose continual interest this book could have been finished in half the time. You are my inspiration and pleasure treasure.

I want to acknowledge my Guru Dr. M. S. Prasad for being there in my life. I just cannot imagine my life without him. My meagre understanding of my domain is nothing in front of the ocean of knowledge in his possession. Thanks a lot for giving me a chance to observe and learn from you. You are the idol for me. I request Lord Shree Krishna to give me character and courage to follow on the footsteps of you.

I am grateful to my Boss Dr. Apoorva Palkar for providing an excellent academic and research-oriented atmosphere in the Sinhgad Institute of Management and Computer Application (SIMCA), Pune. You are and will remain as an inspiration and benchmark of efficiency for me.

I appreciate everyone at Sinhgad Institute of Management and Computer Application (SIMCA), Pune for providing an amazing example of teamwork and coordination. I just could not have been in a position to complete this book without the support from the teaching as well as the non-teaching staff of my institute. One requires a joyous and charged place to work at, and that's exactly what you are responsible for. I am really fortunate to be a part of your team.

I want to acknowledge everyone at Himalaya Publishing House Pvt. Ltd. who contributed to help me produce this book. Especially I would like to thank Mr. Santosh and Mr. Surendra for having faith in me.

Finally, I give the ultimate thanks to Lord Shree Krishna. He is the source of everything. I am thankful for the gifts given to me by Him. I don't deserve his mercy, but am immensely grateful for having received it. I request him to mercifully grant me opportunities to share it with the others.

Hare Krishna Hare Krishna, Krishna Krishna Hare Hare I
Hare Rama Hare Rama, Rama Rama Hare Hare II

Authors

Contents

Section-VI: Puzzles in C

Section-VII: Objective Tests on C Language

Detailed Contents

Section-I: A Brief Overview of C Language

Section-II: Processing and Execution of a C Program

Section-III: Utilities and Tools to Process a C Program

SECTION

I: A BRIEF OVERVIEW OF C LANGUAGE

Objectives

This section is a short refresher course on C language. Prior experience with C programming is expected here. This section does not intend to teach the C language. It takes an overview of the C language at an advanced level.

Contents:

CHAPTER

1 A Brief Overview of C Language

1.1: A BRIEF HISTORY OF C LANGUAGE

In the early days of computers, the only programming languages available to programmers were two "low level" languages: machine and assembly language. Programming in these languages was tedious and time-consuming because the programmer had to manage the hardware itself (memory, stack, interrupts, etc.). When computers became increasingly available, many "high level" languages such as Fortran, Pascal, and Basic were developed in order to make the underlying hardware invisible to the programmer and to make syntax easier; thereby making computers easier and faster to program.

In 1972, the Unix Operating System was being developed. During this time, the concept of a system programming language having attributes of both "low level" and "high level" languages also developed. System programming languages have advantages of a high level language but allow the programmer to take control of the underlying hardware if desired.

Brian W. Kernigahn and Dennis M. Ritchie developed C at Bell Laboratories as a system programming language. Their underlying goal was to develop a language that was simple and flexible enough to be used in a variety of different processors. (Two early versions were named A and B.) In 1983, the American National Standards Institute formed a committee to produce a C programming language standard. This "ANSI C" was completed in 1988. Throughout its history, C has been closely associated with the UNIX operating system, with system programming in general, and with the challenge of writing "portable" code that can be easily transferred to any one of many target computers.

In recent years, several variants of C have developed, e.g., C++ (C with objects) is one of the most popular programming languages in the world. Small C is widely used for micro-controllers.

This chapter is organised into two sections:

- Building blocks of C language: operators, separators, variables, functions, if/else statements, and loops.
- Create a C program: It includes file structure, pre-processor, variable scope, and library functions.

1.2: BUILDING BLOCKS OF C LANGUAGE

1.2.1: Operators

Operators are used to manipulate data. Operators perform calculations, check for equality, make assignments, and manipulate variables. Of the 40 commonly used operators, following 20 are most commonly used.

<table>
<tr><td colspan="3">Assignment Operators</td></tr>
<tr><td>=</td><td>Assignment</td><td>x = y;</td></tr>
<tr><td colspan="3">Mathematical Operators</td></tr>
<tr><td>+</td><td>Addition</td><td>x = x + y;</td></tr>
<tr><td>-</td><td>Subtraction</td><td>x = x - y;</td></tr>
<tr><td>*</td><td>Multiplication</td><td>x = x*y;</td></tr>
<tr><td>/</td><td>Division</td><td>x = x/y;</td></tr>
<tr><td>%</td><td>Modulus</td><td>x = x %y</td></tr>
<tr><td colspan="3">Logical Operators</td></tr>
<tr><td>&&</td><td>Logical AND</td><td>x = true && false;</td></tr>
<tr><td>||</td><td>Logical OR</td><td>x = true || false;</td></tr>
<tr><td>&</td><td>Bitwise AND</td><td>x = x & 0xFF;</td></tr>
<tr><td>|</td><td>Bitwise OR</td><td>x = x | 0xFF;</td></tr>
<tr><td>~</td><td>Bitwise NOT</td><td>x = x ~ 0xFF;</td></tr>
<tr><td>!</td><td>Logical NOT</td><td>false = !true;</td></tr>
<tr><td>>></td><td>Shift Bits Right</td><td>x = x >> 1;</td></tr>
<tr><td><<</td><td>Shift Bits Left</td><td>x = x << 2;</td></tr>
<tr><td colspan="3">Equality Operators</td></tr>
<tr><td>==</td><td>Equal to</td><td>if(x == 10){...}</td></tr>
<tr><td>!=</td><td>Not Equal to</td><td>if(x != 10){...}</td></tr>
<tr><td><</td><td>Less than</td><td>if(x < 10){...}</td></tr>
<tr><td>></td><td>Greater than</td><td>if(x > 10){...}</td></tr>
<tr><td><=</td><td>Less than or equal to</td><td>if(x <= 10) {...}</td></tr>
<tr><td>>=</td><td>Greater than or equal to</td><td>if(x >= 10){...}</td></tr>
</table>

Note: Mathematical Operators follow standard precedence. Multiplication and division will be executed before any addition or subtraction.

1.2.2: Separators

There are five types of separators needed for this discussion.

{ } These separators are used to group together lines of code and initialise arrays.

;		This separator is used to separate lines of code.
(	)	These separators are used to specify parameters and to change mathematical operator precedence.
		Example: Changing mathematical operator precedence:
		5 + 7 * 2 = 19
		(5 + 7) * 2 = 24
[	]	These separators are used to index arrays.
"	"	These separators indicate a string.
/*	*/	These separators indicate a comment

1.2.3: Data Types

In C a *data type* defines the way the program stores information in memory. The size in bytes a data type uses varies with every development system. So, be careful.

Data Type	Description	Size in Bytes (32 bit system)
void	nothing	0
char	character	1
int	integer	2
long	integer	4
float	floating point	4
double	floating point	8

All of these data types are signed. The most significant bit is used to indicate positive or negative. A *type modifier* "unsigned" can be used to use the most significant bit.

Example:		
int	possible range of values	-32,768 to 32,767
unsigned int	possible range of values	0 to 65,535

Every variable used in a program must be declared.

Example:

```
int myvariable;
```

You can assign an initial value to an array by using the assignment operator.

Example:

```
int myvariable = 5;
```

An ***array*** is a collection of values. An array is allocated using the [] separator.

Example: Declaring an array of integers that holds five values.

int myarray[5];

If you want to assign an initial value to an array, you would use the {} separators.

Example: Filling an array with an initial value.

int myarray[5] = { -300, -400, -2, 4, 5};

If initial values of the array are given, the compiler is smart enough to figure out how many positions are needed to hold the initial values.

Example: Alternative way to declare an array with initial values.

int myarray[] = { -300, -400, -2, 4, 5};

A *string* is an array of character values.

Example: Declaring a string.

char mystring[10];

To initialise a string, the assignment operator and " " separators are used. The compiler will also place a NULL character (NULL = 0) at the end of the string to indicate the end of a string.

Example: Initialising a string.

char mystring[] = "Hello";

To use a particular value or character in an array you can index the value using the [] separators.

Note: Index of an array starts at 0

Example: Indexing

myarray[2] from above is equal to -2

mystring[1] from above is equal to 'e'

1.2.4: Functions

Functions are the building blocks of a C program. Functions are sections of code that perform a single, well-defined service. All executable code in C is within a function. Functions take any number of parameters and return a maximum of 1 value. A parameter is a value passed to a function that is used to alter its operation or indicate the extent of its operations. A function in C looks like this:

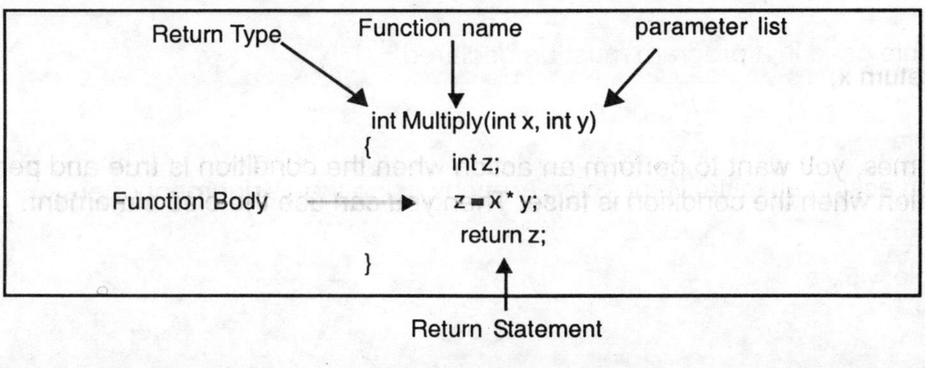

In the data type section, you might have wondered what the "void" type was used for. If a function does not return a value or there are no parameters, the type void is used.

Example:

```
void PrintHello(void)
{
printf("Hello World");      /* printf prints a string to the screen*/
return;
}
```

Another question you might ask is which function is executed first in a program. In C the function named "main" is executed first.

Like variables, all functions except the "main" function must be declared before it is defined.

Example: Declaring a function

```
void PrintHello(void);
```

> **Note:** An array as a parameter has this form in the declaration: void ArrayFunction(int SomeArray[]);
> Then when calling the function, give the function the array's name: int MyArray[10];
> ArrayFunction(MyArray);

1.2.5: Conditional Constructs

The if statement is a conditional statement. If the condition given to the if statement is true then a section of code is executed.

Syntax: if(*condition*)

```
        {
        execute this code if condition is true
        }
```

Example:

```
int absolute(int x)
{
    if(x < 0)
        {
            x = -1 * x;
        }
        return x;
}
```

Sometimes, you want to perform an action when the condition is true and perform a different action when the condition is false. Then you can use the else statement.

Syntax:

```
if(condition)
    {
    execute this code if condition is true
    }
else
    {
    execute this code if condition is false
    }
```

It is very easy to chain a lot of if/else statements.

Syntax:
```
if(condition 1)
    {
    execute this code if condition 1 is true
    }
else if(condition 2)
    {
    execute this code if condition 1 is false and condition 2 is true
    }
else
    {
    execute this code if condition 1 and condition 2 are false
    }
```

1.2.6: Iteractive Constructs

It has been proven that the only loop needed for programming is the while loop. While the condition given to the while loop is true a section of code is executed.

Syntax:

```
while(condition)
{
        execute this code while the condition is true
}
```

Example:

```
unsigned int factorial(unsigned int x)
{
        unsigned int result;
        while(x > 0)
        {
                result = result*x;
                x = x -1;
        }
        return result;
}
```

You can break out of a while loop prematurely by using the break statement.

Example:

```
int x = 0;
 while (true)
{
   if(x == 10000)
   {
         break;
   }
   x = x + 1
}
```

In this example the condition given to the while loop is always true. Once x equals 10000 the program will exit the while loop.

The other major loop is the for loop. It takes three parameters: the starting number the test condition that determines when the loop stops and the increment expression.

Syntax:

for(*initial; condition; adjust*)

{

code to be executed while the condition is true

}

The for loop repeatedly executes a section of code while the condition is true. The statement *initial* initialises the state of the loop. After the section of code is executed, the state is modified using the statement *adjust*.

Example:

```
unsigned int factorial( unsigned x)
{
        int counter;
        unsigned int result = 1;
        for( counter = 1; counter <= x; counter = counter + 1)
        {
        result = result*x;
        }
         return result;
}
```

1.3: CREATE A C PROGRAM

1.3.1: File Types

Every C compiler adheres to certain "rules" regarding file extensions.

.c:

These are C source files. They usually contain only functions and pre-processor commands with one exception. Any C source file containing the function "main" also includes global variable declarations for variables used in the file and function declarations for functions defined in the file.

.h:

Every C source file without the "main" function has a header file with the same name. The header file includes pre-processor commands, global variable declarations for variables used in the associated C source file, and function declarations for functions defined in the associated C source file.

.o:

After the compiler "compiles" the C source file, an object file with the same name is created. This is done primarily to save the compiler time. The compiler will only compile files that have recently been changed.

.lib:

If the source file will never change then the programmer can create a library file. The programmer can then use the functions in the library file. The "main" function is not allowed in a library file.

.exe:

This is the only file extension that varies from system-to-system. When a user compiles a program, a compiler creates object files from the source files. Then a linker links any functions used in the object files together to create an executable file.

1.3.2: Library Functions

C development packages always contain standard libraries. In essence, standard functions are provided to the programmer.

1.3.2.1: Standard Input/Output Functions

int printf(const char *format[, argument, ...]);

- Accepts a series of arguments
- Applies to each argument a format specifier contained in the format string *format
- Outputs the formatted data to the screen.

To use this function, we have to give it the name of a character array or a string itself.

Example: Printing a string array.

char myString[] = "Hello World";

printf(myString);

Example: Printing with an actual string.

printf("Hello World");

Using arguments and ***format specifiers***, we can print a variable's value to the screen. Format specifiers can vary between development systems.

Format Specifiers		
%d	Integer	signed decimal integer
%i	Integer	signed decimal integer
%o	Integer	unsigned octal integer
%u	Integer	unsigned decimal integer
%x	Integer	unsigned hexadecimal int (with a, b, c, d, e, f)
%X	Integer	unsigned hexadecimal int (with A, B, C, D, E, F)
%f	Floating point	signed value
%c	Character	Single character
%s	String pointer	Prints characters until a null-terminator
%%	None	Prints the % character

Example: Printing a variable's value

int x = 5;

int y = x*x;

printf("%d squared equals %d",x,y);

The above example will print "5 squared equals 25" onto the screen.

To display non-graphical characters (such as a new-line character) and separators, an ***escape sequence*** is needed.

Escape Sequences		
\n	LF	Newline (linefeed)
\r	CR	Carriage return
\t	HT	Tab (horizontal)
\\	\	Backslash
\'	'	Single quote (apostrophe)
\"	"	Double quote
\?	?	Question mark

int scanf(const char *format[, address, ...]);

- scans a series of input fields one character at a time
- formats each field according to a corresponding format specifier passed in the format string.

Scanf is similar to printf. It is used to obtain user input. There must be at least one address argument. To get an address argument use the '&' operator in front of variable names but not in front of character arrays. (the '&' operator is an "address of" operator.)

Example: Entering a number

```
int x;
printf("Please input an integer:");
 scanf("%d",&x);
```

Example: Entering a string

```
int char buffer[80];
printf("Please input a string");
scanf("%s",buffer);
```

1.3.2.2: Standard Mathematical Functions

There are many functions in the math library to do standard mathematical operations such as: sin, cos, tangent, exponent, log, etc. You can look at the associated header file "math.h" to find out the parameter list and return type for each function.

There are also non-mathematical functions in the math library. These functions are used to convert a string into an integer or floating point value. These are not required for this discussion.

1.3.3: Pre-processor

Pre-processor directives are instructions for the compiler. Pre-processor directives are prefixed by the '#' character. For this discussion only two different pre-processor commands are needed.

```
#include <filename.h>
```

The include directive is used to link C source files, object files, and library files together. For this discussion we will use this to link the library files. This directive must appear before global variable declarations and function declarations.

```
#define NAME VALUE
```

The define directive is used to set definitions.

Example:

```
#define PI 3.14
```

1.3.4: Calling a Function

We should say a little more about the mechanism by which an argument is passed to a function. Formally, C is call by value, which means that a function receives copies of the values of its parameters. Suppose we create a function that multiplies a number by 2.

```
int multtwo(int x)
{
   x = x * 2;
   return x;
}
```

We might wonder, if we wrote it this way, what would happen to the value of the variable z if we write this code.

```
z = 5
j = multtwo(z);
```

When our implementation of multtwo changes the value of x, does that change the value of z when we use it as a parameter? The answer is no. x receives a copy of z's value, so when we change x we don't change z.

There is an exception to this rule. When the argument passed to a function is an array, the function does not receive a copy of the array, and it, therefore, can modify the array. So how do we change multiple values with a single function? We can put all of our variables in array form, but that is not a very elegant solution. The elegant way to solve this problem is to use pointers but since we will not be using pointers in our discussion, we turn to variable scope.

Levels:

```
Base Level
{
Level 1 a: inside a function
        {
        Level 2a
        }
        {
        Level 2b
        }
}
{
Level 1 b: inside a function
}
```

It is clear that levels are separated by the {} separator. Any variable declared in a level is only available to higher numbered levels. If a variable is declared in Level 1a, only Level 2a, and Level 2b will have access to the variable. If a variable is declared in Level 2a, Level 2b will not have access to that variable because it is not a higher numbered level.

If we declare a variable in the Base Level then it becomes a global variable. Any functions defined in the same file will be able to use that variable. This is how we get functions to change multiple variables.

1.3.5: A Complete C Program

With all of the information you gained above and perusing some library header files, you should be able to put together a functional C program. To illustrate, here is a program to convert an integer to binary.

```
/*
Example:Integer to binary conversion
*/
/* Pre-processor directives come first*/
#include <stdio.h>
/* global variables and function declarations come next*/
int IntToBinary(int x, int bin[]);
```

void main(void)	
{	
int x;	/* Declare an integer variable */
int limit;	/* Declare an integer variable */
int binaryarray[20];	/* Declare an integer array */

```
/* Let the user input a variable and make sure it is positive*/ while(true)
{
printf("\n Input a positive integer:"); scanf("%d",&x);
if(x < 0)
    {
printf("\n Not a positive integer");
    }
else
    {
break;
    }
    }
/* Call the Int to Binary function to store the bits in binaryarray */
limit = IntToBinary(x,binaryarray);
/* Now print the contents of the binary array. Note I declare counter in for's parameter list.
        This means that this variable is only accessible in the for loop */
for(int counter = 0; counter < limit; counter = counter + 1)
    {
printf("\n Bit %d is %d",counter,binaryarray[counter]);
    }
/* End the program*/
return;
}
```

```
/* Now define the function IntToBinary */
int IntToBinary(int x, int bin[])
    {
int counter = 0;
while( x > 0 )
        {
if((x%2) != 0)
        {
        bin[counter] = 1;
        }
else
        {
        bin[counter] = 0;
}
x = x / 2;
counter = counter + 1;
}
return counter;
}
```

SECTION

SECTION-II: PROCESSING AND EXECUTION OF A C PROGRAM

Objectives

This section deals with mostly neglected aspects of C programming; namely processing and execution of a C program. Generally, a C programmer never bothers about the background activities involved in the processing of a C program. The conversion process of C source code file(s) to the final executable file is a fascinating process. A thorough understanding of the same gives the programmers a better understanding of the C language and provides intellectual satisfaction. The execution of the resultant executable is also shrouded in mystery. A thorough understanding of the binary contents of an executable file provides the insight into this. The chapters from this section will unravel these mysteries.

Contents:

CHAPTER

2 Steps Involved in the Processing of a C Program

2.1: INTRODUCTION TO THE PROCESSING OF A C PROGRAM

There is a little bit of confusion about C language. Whether to call it a HLL (High-Level-Language) or a MLL (Middle-Level-Language)? This confusion stems from the 'realised' power of C. The general notion says that; more flexible the development tools are, more powerful the language is. This perfectly applies to the C language also.

When we are talking about a development environment for a language, we are talking about the applications/utilities, which make the conversion of textual source file in that language into an executable file possible. It also includes the utilities, which make writing of the source code easier, as well as the utilities, which help us to debug the executable.

Generally, a programmer calls the compiler program to process a C source code file. This gives an illusion that the compilation is a one step process. In reality, the C program processing is a multi-step activity. The C programming toolkit contains a dedicated utility/tool for each of these activities. The program, which a programmer calls the so-called compiler, is just a driver program which calls other utilities in a predefined order.

E.g., on Linux platform a programmer calls 'gcc' to process a C program. In reality, 'gcc' is not a compiler at all! gcc is a program which calls other programs. It's a program that chains different programs by means of temporary files created in /tmp directory. Same is true with all the other compilers.

A generic C program processing process involves a four-step approach towards C processing procedure:

1. First it pre-processes the source code.
2. Then it compiles this 'actual' source code into its corresponding assembly language code.
3. This resultant assembly language code is then assembled into corresponding object code.
4. Finally this object code is then linked with operating system-dependent wrapper code and standard library code to generate the final executable code.

We can summarise the involved steps in the following diagram:

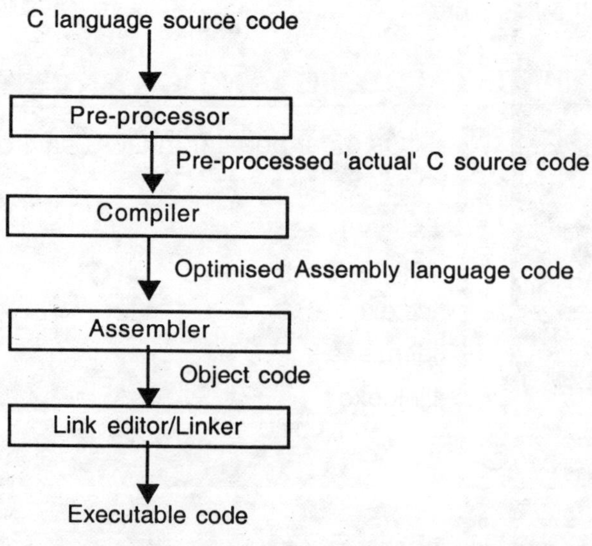

2.2: THE ORGANISATION OF A GENERIC C PROGRAMMING TOOLKIT

A generic C programming toolkit contains a dedicated utility/tool for each of the mentioned steps in the C language processing.

A Source Code Editor:

A Source Code Editor enables the creation of a C source code file. It supports ASCII and Unicode. A Source code editor is different from a word processor.

A Pre-processor:

A Pre-processor deals with all the pre-processing directives. It makes appropriate changes in the original source code according to the respective directives. The output of a pre-processor contains pure C source code.

A Compiler:

A Compiler converts the C source code into its corresponding assembly code. Source code optimisation is taken care of in this stage.

An Assembler:

An Assembler compiles the assembly source code into the machine-dependent object code. It packages the object code depending upon the operating system in use.

A Linker:

A Linker combines the different object code files with required library files. Output of the Linker is an executable program.

A Debugger:

A Debugger helps the programmer to remove programming errors.

An Integrated Development Environment (IDE):

An IDE provides an easy-to-use interface for the programmer. It makes all the involved utilities readily available to the programmer.

2.3: C PROGRAMMING TOOLKIT IN DOS ENVIRONMENT

The Turbo C/C++ 3.0 toolkit is most popular in DOS environment. Its organisation is as follows:

Source Code Editor	:	edit.com
Pre-processor	:	cpp.exe
Compiler	:	tcc.exe
Assembler	:	tasm.exe
Linker	:	tlink.exe

2.4: C PROGRAMMING TOOLKIT IN WINDOWS ENVIRONMENT

The Visual C++ 6.0 toolkit is most popular in Windows environment. Its organisation is as follows:

Source Code Editor : notepad.exe
Pre-processor : cpp.exe
Compiler : cl.exe
Assembler : masm.exe
Linker : link.exe

2.5: C PROGRAMMING TOOLKIT IN LINUX ENVIRONMENT

The 'gcc' toolkit is most popular in Linux environment. Its organisation is as follows:

Source Code Editor : vi editor, emacs editor
Pre-processor : /usr/bin/cpp
Compiler : /usr/lib/gcc-lib/i386-redhat-linux/2.96/cc1 (distribution specific path)
Assembler : /usr/bin/as
Linker : /usr/bin/ld
Debugger : /usr/bin/gdb

CHAPTER

3 Understanding the Processing of a C Program

As we have seen in the discussion concerning the C programming toolkit, generally, a programmer calls the compiler program to process a C source-code file. This gives an illusion that the compilation is a one-step process. In reality, the C program processing is a multi-step activity. The C programming toolkit contains a dedicated utility/tool for each of these activities. The program, which a programmer calls (the so-called compiler), is just a driver program which calls other utilities in a pre-defined order.

In our further discussion we are going to concentrate upon the conversion process of source code into the executable code. We will see in detail, how the entire toolkit contributes towards the processing of a C program.

We will try to understand these steps in detail with an example. We will use the previous example, having the files our_header.h and add.c.

As a case study, we will be using the 'gcc' toolkit on Linux platform. The discussion applies to the other toolkits and environments with some minor changes.

3.1: PRE-PROCESSING

In the pre-processing step, the header files are included and the macroinstructions are replaced appropriately. The user-created source file gets modified and expanded to produce the 'actual' source file.

'/usr/bin/cpp' program (C Pre-processor) is used to perform this step. It's basically a text manipulation program and we can write our own limited version of it very easily.

```
$cpp add.c -o add.i
$
$cat add.i
  # 1 "add.c"
  # 1 "our_include.h" 1
  # 2 "add.c" 2
  main()
 {
            int C;
            C = 10 + 20;
            printf("%d\n", C);
 }
$
```

Step: Pre-processing

Utility program: /usr/bin/cpp

Input file: add.c

Output file: add.i

3.2: COMPILATION

In the compilation step, the 'actual' source code is compiled into corresponding optimised assembly language code. It also indicates the occurrences of syntax errors, if any.

'/usr/lib/gcc-lib/i386-redhat-linux/2.96/cc1' program (C Compiler-1) is used to perform this step. This program performs the lexical, syntactical and semantic analysis on the 'actual' source code. For any occurrences of lexical or syntactical errors it may generate error messages and for any occurrences of semantic errors it may generate warning messages. In case of no errors it will generate corresponding optimised assembly code. The cc1 program generates AT&T syntax-style assembly code.

```
$/usr/lib/gcc-lib/i386-redhat-linux/2.96/cc1 add.i -o add.s
$
$cat add.s
        .file "add.c"
        .version "01.01"
 gcc2_compiled.:
        .section .rodata
 .LC0:
        .string    "%d\n"
 .text
        .align 4
 .globl main
        .type     main,@function
 main:
        pushl    %ebp
        movl     %esp, %ebp
        subl     $8, %esp
        movl     $30, -4(%ebp)
        subl     $8, %esp
        pushl    -4(%ebp)
        pushl    $.LC0
        call      printf
       addl $16, %esp
       leave
       ret
 .Lfe1:
 .size        main,.Lfe1-main
 .ident    "GCC:(GNU)2.96 20000731(Red Hat Linux 7.1 2.96-81)"
$
```

Step: Compilation

Utility program: /usr/lib/gcc-lib/i386-redhat-linux/2.96/cc1

Input file: add.i

Output file: add.s

3.3: ASSEMBLY

In the assembly step, the assembly language code is assembled into the corresponding object code. In this step, the processing domain changes from textual to binary. Before this step, the input and output files, both were in simple ASCII text format. But this step produces a binary object file as its output by taking the assembly text file as its input.

'/usr/bin/as' program (Assembler) is used to perform this step. This program performs the lexical, syntactical and semantic analysis on the assembly language source code. For any occurrences of lexical or syntactical errors it may generate error messages and for any occurrences of semantic errors it may generate warning messages. In case of no errors it will generate corresponding optimized object code. As in this case the assembly code is going to be written by the cc1 program itself, there won't be any errors in it giving us the object code directly.

```
$as add.s -o add.o
$
$ls
  add.c add.i add.o add.s our_include.h
$
```

Step: Assembly

Utility program: /usr/bin/as

Input file: add.s

Output file: add.o

3.4: LINKING

In the linking step, the executable code is generated by grouping all the object files and editing of the links. This is the most complex step in the whole process as it requires quite a few parameters to be considered.

As the GNU development environment is also used for the object-oriented languages like C++ and Objecive-C, it has to consider the object-oriented approach also. In object-oriented languages a compiler require to create constructor and destructor methods, which execute before and after the execution of 'main'. To facilitate this, the GNU development model embeds user code within a wrapper of system code. This approach treats the 'main' as a function call. Advantage of this is that the user is not required to initialise the environment, though user code must obey some function requirements.

'/usr/bin/ld' program (Link eDitor) is used to perform the linking step. This program groups the architecture-dependent prefix-code, the initialisation wrapper code, standard C library code, actual program code and the cleanup wrapper code to produce the final executable code. While grouping the codes it resolves the symbols as well.

```
$ld -m elf_i386 -dynamic-linker /lib/ld-linux.so.2 /usr/lib/crt1.o /usr/lib/crti.o /usr/lib/gcc-lib/i386-redhat-linux/2.96/crtbegin.o-L/usr/lib-lc add.o/usr/lib/gcc-lib/i386-redhat-linux/2.96/crtend.o/usr/lib/crtn.o
$ls
 add add.c add.i add.o add.s our_include.h
$
$./add
 30
$
```

The '-m elf_i386' option instructs the link editor to create executable code for i386 platform in ELF, Executable and Linking Format, binary format.

The '-dynamic-linker' option instructs the link editor to link the libraries dynamically to the resultant code. Here we are dynamically linking the standard C library, libc.so, to the resultant executable code.

Step: Linking

Utility program: /usr/bin/ld

Input files:

architecture dependent prefix code: /lib/ld-linux.so.2

initialization code: /usr/lib/crt1.o, /usr/lib/crti.o, /usr/lib/gcc-lib/i386-redhat-linux/2.96/crtbegin.o

standard C library: /usr/lib/libc.so

actual object code: add.o

cleanup code: /usr/lib/gcc-lib/i386-redhat-linux/2.96/crtend.o, /usr/lib/crtn.o

Output file: add

CHAPTER

4 Understanding the Execution of a C Program

4.1: INTRODUCTION

The execution of a C program is always considered as a mystery. How a C executable loads into the memory, how the command line parameters are passed to the main() function, how the operating system starts the executing from the main() function, etc., are a few of the points to understand in order to unravel this mystery.

In this chapter, we will use the following program to illustrate these concepts. It is called "simple.c". As already we have dissected all the steps involved in the C program processing (from source code to executable) in previous chapter, using Linux environment as a case study, we will use the same environment here. The discussion is valid for other environments with some minor changes.

```
/* simple.c */
main()
{
    return(0);
}
```

Build the above file using the following command:

```
gcc -o simple simple.c
```

4.2: UNDERSTANDING AN EXECUTABLE

To see what's in the executable, let's use a tool "objdump"

```
objdump -f simple
simple:        file format elf32-i386
architecture: i386, flags 0x00000112:
EXEC_P, HAS_SYMS, D_PAGED
start address 0x080482d0
```

The output gives us some critical information about the executable.

First of all, the file is "ELF32" format. Second, the start address is "0x080482d0"

4.3: EXECUTABLE FILE FORMAT

ELF is acronym for Executable and Linking Format. It is one of several object and executable file formats used on Unix systems. For our discussion, the interesting thing about ELF is its header format. Every ELF executable has ELF header, which is the following.

```
typedef    struct
{
           unsigned char    e_ident[EI_NIDENT];   /* Magic number and other info */
           Elf32_Half       e_type;               /* Object file type */
           Elf32_Half       e_machine;            /* Architecture */
           Elf32_Word       e_version;            /* Object file version */
           Elf32_Addr       e_entry;              /* Entry point virtual address */
           Elf32_Off        e_phoff;              /* Program header table file offset */
           Elf32_Off        e_shoff;              /* Section header table file offset */
           Elf32_Word       e_flags;              /* Processor-specific flags */
           Elf32_Half       e_ehsize;             /* ELF header size in bytes */
           Elf32_Half       e_phentsize;          /* Program header table entry size */
           Elf32_Half       e_phnum;              /* Program header table entry count */
           Elf32_Half       e_shentsize;          /* Section header table entry size */
           Elf32_Half       e_shnum;              /* Section header table entry count */
           Elf32_Half       e_shstrndx;           /* Section header string table index */
                                                  } Elf32_Ehdr;
```

In the above structure, there is "e_entry" field, which is starting address of an executable.

4.4: STARTING ADDRESS OF AN EXECUTABLE FILE

For this question, let's disassemble "simple". There are several tools to disassemble an executable. I/we shall use objdump for this purpose.

objdump --disassemble simple

The output is a little bit long so I/we shall not paste all the output from objdump. Our intention is to see what is at address 0x080482d0. Here is the output.

```
080482d0 <_start>:
 80482d0:    31 ed              xor     %ebp,%ebp
 80482d2:    5e                 pop     %esi
 80482d3:    89 e1              mov     %esp,%ecx
 80482d5:    83 e4 f0           and     $0xfffffff0,%esp
 80482d8:    50                 push    %eax
 80482d9:    54                 push    %esp
 80482da:    52                 push    %edx
 80482db:    68 20 84 04 08     push    $0x8048420
 80482e0:    68 74 82 04 08     push    $0x8048274
 80482e5:    51                 push    %ecx
```

```
80482e6:     56                   push    %esi
80482e7:     68 d0 83 04 08       push    $0x80483d0
80482ec:     e8 cb ff ff ff       call    80482bc <_init+0x48>
80482f1:     f4                   hlt
80482f2:     89 f6           mov  %esi,%esi
```

Looks like some kind of starting routine called "_start" is at the starting address. What it does is clear a register, push some values into stack and call a function. According to this instruction, the stack frame should look like this.

```
Stack Top  -------------------
           0x80483d
           -------------------
           esi
           -------------------
           ecx
           -------------------
           0x8048274
           -------------------
           0x8048420
           -------------------
           edx
           -------------------
           esp
           -------------------
           eax
           -------------------
```

Now, as you already wonder, we have got a few questions regarding this stack frame.

1. What are those hex values about?
2. What is at address 80482bc, which is called by _start?
3. Looks like the assembly instructions do not initialise any register with possibly meaningful values. Then who initialises the registers?

Let us answer these questions one-by-one.

The HEX Values:

If you look at disassembled output from objdump carefully, you can answer this question easily.

Here is the answer.

0x80483d0 : This is the address of our main() function.

0x8048274 : _init function.

0x8048420 : _fini function _init and _fini is initialisation/finalisation functic provided by GCC.

Right now, let us not worry about these details. Basically, all those hexa values are function pointers.

Address 80482bc:

Again, let us look for address 80482bc from the disassembly output.

If you look for it, the assembly is

80482bc: ff 25 48 95 04 08 jmp *0x8049548

Here, *0x8049548 is a pointer operation.

It just jumps to an address stored at address 0x8049548.

4.5: UNDERSTANDING THE DYNAMIC LINKING

With ELF, we can build an executable linked dynamically with libraries.

Here, "linked dynamically" means the actual linking process happens at runtime. Otherwise, we would have to build a huge executable containing all the libraries it calls (a "statically-linked executable). If you issue the command:

"ldd simple"

libc.so.6 => /lib/i686/libc.so.6 (0x42000000)

/lib/ld-linux.so.2 => /lib/ld-linux.so.2 (0x40000000)

You can see all the libraries dynamically linked with simple. All the dynamically linked data and functions have "dynamic relocation entry".

The concept is roughly like this.

1. We don't know actual address of a dynamic symbol at link time. We can know the actual address of the symbol only at runtime.
2. So, for the dynamic symbol, we reserve a memory location for the actual address. The memory location will be filled with actual address of the symbol at runtime by loader.
3. Our application sees the dynamic symbol indirectly with the memory location by using kind of pointer operation. In our case, at address 80482bc, there is just a simple jump instruction. And the jump location is stored at address 0x8049548 by loader during runtime. We can see all dynamic link entries with objdump command.

```
objdump -R simple
    simple:     file format elf32-i386

    DYNAMIC RELOCATION RECORDS
    OFFSET   TYPE              VALUE
    0804954c R_386_GLOB_DAT    __gmon_start__
    08049540 R_386_JUMP_SLOT   __register_frame_info
    08049544 R_386_JUMP_SLOT   __deregister_frame_info
    08049548 R_386_JUMP_SLOT   __libc_start_main
```

Here, address 0x8049548 is called "jump slot", which perfectly makes sense. And according to the table, actually we want to call __libc_start_main.

__libc_start_main function:

Now the ball is on libc's hand. __libc_start_main is a function in libc.so.6. If you look for __libc_start_main in glibc source code, the prototype looks like this.

```
extern int BP_SYM (__libc_start_main) (int (*main) (int, char **, char **),
        int argc,
        char *__unbounded *__unbounded ubp_av,
        void (*init) (void),
        void (*fini) (void),
        void (*rtld_fini) (void),
        void *__unbounded stack_end)
__attribute__ ((noreturn));
```

And all the assembly instructions do is set up argument stack and call __libc_start_main.

What this function does is set up/initialise some data structures/environments and call our main(). Let us look at the stack frame with this function prototype.

```
Stack Top  -------------------
           0x80483d0          main
           -------------------
           esi                argc
           -------------------
           ecx                argv
           -------------------
           0x8048274          _init
           -------------------
           0x8048420          _fini
```

```
-------------------
edx                        _rtlf_fini
-------------------
esp                        stack_end
-------------------
eax                        this is 0
-------------------
```

According to this stack frame, esi, ecx, edx, esp, eax registers should be filled with appropriate values before __libc_start_main() is executed. Clearly these registers are not set by the startup assembly instructions shown before. Then, who sets these registers? Now I guess the only thing left. The kernel.

Now let us go back to our third question.

4.6: UNDERSTANDING THE ROLE OF OPERATING SYSTEM KERNEL

When we execute a program by entering a name on shell, this is what happens in Linux.

1. The shell calls the kernel system call "execve" with argc/argv.
2. The kernel system call handler gets control and start handling the system call. In kernel code, the handler is "sys_execve". On x86, the user-mode application passes all required parameters to kernel with the following registers.
   - ebx : pointer to program name string
   - ecx : argv array pointer
   - edx : environment variable array pointer.
3. The generic execve kernel system call handler, which is do_execve, is called. What it does is, set up a data structure and copy some data from user space to kernel space and finally calls search_binary_handler(). Linux can support more than one executable file format such as a.out and ELF at the same time. For this functionality, there is a data structure "struct linux_binfmt", which has a function pointer for each binary format loader. And search_binary_handler() just looks up an appropriate handler and calls it. In our case, load_elf_binary() is the handler. To explain each detail of the function would be lengthy/boring work. So I will not do that. If you are interested in it, read a book about it. As a picture tells a thousand words, a thousand lines of source code tells ten thousand words (sometimes). Here is the bottom line of the function. It first sets up kernel data structures for file operation to read the ELF executable image in. Then it sets up a kernel data structure: code size, data segment start, stack segment start, etc., and it allocates user mode pages for this process and copies the argv and environment variables to those allocated page addresses. Finally, argc, the argv pointer, and the environment variable array pointer are pushed to user mode stack by create_elf_tables(), and start_thread() starts the process execution rolling.

When the _start assembly instruction gets control of execution, the stack frame looks like this.

```
Stack Top      -------------
                  argc
               -------------
                  argv pointer
               -------------
                  env pointer
               -------------
```

And the assembly instructions gets all information from stack by

```
pop %esi            <--- get argc
move %esp, %ecx          <--- get argv
                 actually the argv address is the same as the current
                 stack pointer.
```

And now we are all set to start executing.

4.7: INVOLVEMENT OF THE PROCESSOR REGISTERS

For esp, this is used for stack end in application program. After popping all necessary information, the _start routine simply adjusts the stack pointer (esp) by turning off lower 4 bits from esp register. This perfectly makes sense since actually, to our main program, that is the end of stack. For edx, which is used for rtld_fini, a kind of application destructor, the kernel just sets it to 0 with the following macro.

```
#define ELF_PLAT_INIT(_r)  do { \
    _r->ebx = 0; _r->ecx = 0; _r->edx = 0; \
    _r->esi = 0; _r->edi = 0; _r->ebp = 0; \
    _r->eax = 0; \
} while (0)
```

The 0 means we don't use that functionality on x86 linux.

4.8: LOCATION OF THE SUPPORTING CODE

All the discussed supporting code is a part of GCC code. You can usually find all the object files for the code at /usr/lib/gcc-lib/i386-redhat-linux/XXX and /usr/lib where XXX is GCC version. File names are crtbegin.o,crtend.o, gcrt1.o.

4.9: THE BIG PICTURE

1. GCC build your program with crtbegin.o/crtend.o/gcrt1.o And the other default libraries are dynamically linked by default. Starting address of the executable is set to that of _start.
2. Kernel loads the executable and sets up text/data/bss/stack, especially, kernel allocates page(s) for arguments and environment variables and pushes all necessary information on stack.
3. Control is passed to _start. _start gets all information from stack set up by kernel, sets up argument stack for __libc_start_main, and calls it.
4. __libc_start_main initialises necessary stuffs, especially C library (such as malloc) and thread environment and calls our main.
5. Our main is called with main (argv, argv). Actually, here one interesting point is the signature of main. __libc_start_main thinks main's signature as main (int, char **, char **) If you are curious, try the following program.

```
main(int argc, char** argv, char** env)
{
    int i = 0;
    while(env[i] != 0)
    {
        printf("%s\n", env[i++]);
    }
    return(0);
}
```

Thus, in Linux, our C main() function is executed by the cooperative work of GCC, libc and Linux's binary loader.

SECTION

III: UTILITIES AND TOOLS TO PROCESS A C PROGRAM

Objectives

In theory, the understanding of C language is independent of the development tools being used by the programmers. But in reality, the tools used by the programmers affect the capability and efficiency of the applications written in C. Numerous Integrated Development Environments (IDEs) are also available to enhance the productivity of a C programmer. The awareness of various C programming toolkits and IDEs is essential for a professional C programmer. Chapters in this section will briefly discuss the popular C programming toolkits and IDEs. Its objective is to provide a glimpse of available options to professional C programmers.

Contents:

CHAPTER

5 C Programming Toolkits

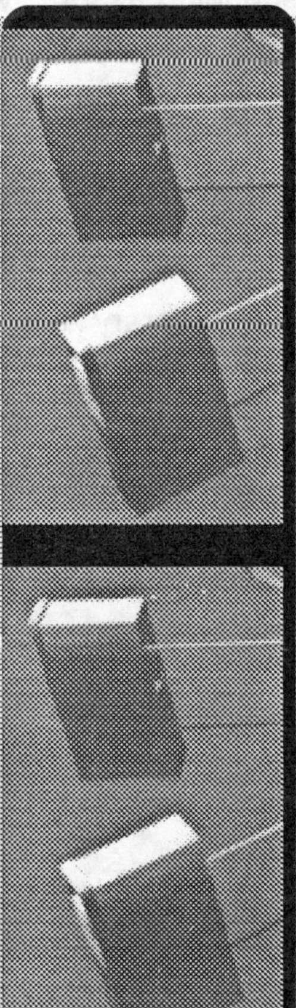

A generic C programming toolkit contains a dedicated utility/tool for each of the steps in the C language processing.

5.1: THE ORGANISATION OF A GENERIC C PROGRAMMING TOOLKIT

A Source Code Editor:

A Source Code Editor enables the creation of a C source code file. It supports ASCII and Unicode. A Source Code Editor is different from a word processor.

A Pre-processor:

A Pre-processor deals with all the pre-processing directives. It makes appropriate changes in the original source code according to the respective directives. The output of a pre-processor contains pure C source code.

A Compiler:

A Compiler converts the C source code into its corresponding assembly code. Source code optimisation is taken care of in this stage.

An Assembler:

An Assembler compiles the assembly source code into the machine-dependent object code. It packages the object code depending upon the operating system in use.

A Linker:

A Linker combines the different object code files with required library files. Output of the Linker is an executable program.

A Debugger:

A Debugger helps the programmer to remove programming errors.

5.2: THE C PROGRAMMING TOOLKITS IN POPULAR ENVIRONMENTS

5.2.1: The C Programming Toolkits in DOS Environment

The Turbo C/C++ 3.0 toolkit is most popular in DOS environment. Its organisation is as follows:

Source Code Editor	:	edit.com
Pre-processor	:	cpp.exe
Compiler	:	tcc.exe
Assembler	:	tasm.exe
Linker	:	tlink.exe

5.2.2: The C Programming Toolkits in Windows Environment

The Visual C++ 6.0 toolkit is most popular in Windows environment. Its organisation is as follows:

Source Code Editor : notepad.exe
Pre-processor : cpp.exe
Compiler : cl.exe
Assembler : masm.exe
Linker : link.exe

5.2.3: The C Programming Toolkits in Linux Environment

The 'GCC' toolkit is most popular in Linux environment. Its organisation is as follows:

Source Code Editor : vi editor, emacs editor
Pre-processor : /usr/bin/cpp
Compiler : /usr/lib/gcc-lib/i386-redhat-linux/2.96/cc1 (distribution specific path)
Assembler : /usr/bin/as
Linker : /usr/bin/ld
Debugger : /usr/bin/gdb

5.3: COMPARISON OF C PROGRAMMING TOOLKITS

Compiler	Author	Platform			License type	IDE
		Windows	UNIX	Other		
Borland C++	CodeGear (Borland)	Yes	No	DOS	Proprietary	Yes
GCC	GNU	Yes	Yes	Yes	Open source	No
Intel C++ Compiler	Intel	Yes	Yes	Yes	Proprietary	Yes
Local C Compiler	Chris Fraser Rand David Hanson	Yes	Yes	Yes	Open source	Windows
Watcom C Compiler	Sybase	Yes	No	Yes	Open source	Yes
TenDRA Compiler	TenDRA Project	No	Yes	No	Open source	No
Tiny C Compiler	Fabrice Bellard	Yes	Yes	No	Open source	No
Visual Studio	Microsoft	Yes	No	No	Proprietary	Yes
Visual Age	IBM	No	Yes	Yes	Proprietary	Yes

5.4: FEATURES OF C PROGRAMMING TOOLKITS

As C++ is considered as a superset of C, the current toolkits support both C and C++ language. If a toolkit claims to be for C++ then It is inherent that it can be used for C also.

5.4.1: Borland C++

Borland C++ is a C and C++ programming environment (used to be called an Integrated Development Environment) for DOS, Windows, and Windows NT. As a successor of Turbo C++, it started with a graphical Windows interface even for developing DOS applications. Besides, It is a better debugger. The Turbo Debugger, was written in protected mode DOS.

Libraries:

Object Windows Library (OWL): A set of C++ classes to make it easier to develop professional graphical Windows applications.

Turbo Vision: A set of C++ classes to create professional applications in DOS. Those classes mimic some of the aspects of a Windows applications like: dialog boxes, messages pumps, menus, accelerators, etc.

Add-ons:

Borland Power Pack for DOS: It allows you to create 16- and 32-bit DOS applications using protected mode. Those applications can access a limited scope of the Windows API and call functions in any Windows DLL.

Borland Code-Guard: Once installed and integrated within the IDE, Code-Guard can insert instrumentalisation code in the final executables that can be used to monitor: pointer usage, API calls, how many times some function is called, among other features. If some error is found, a pop-up window appears, the debugger can stop or a log is written to disk. Delivered for 16- and 32-bit applications.

Version History:

- Borland C++ 2.0
- Borland C++ 3.0
- Borland C++ 3.1
- Borland C++ 4.0 (released in 1993)
- Borland C++ 4.01
- Borland C++ 4.02
- Borland C++ 4.5
- Borland C++ 4.51
- Borland C++ 4.52
- Borland C++ 5.0
- Borland C++ 5.01
- Borland C++ 5.02
- Borland C++ 5.5

5.4.2: GNU Compiler Collection

The GNU Compiler Collection (usually shortened to GCC) is a set of programming language compilers produced by the GNU Project. It is free software distributed by the Free Software Foundation (FSF) under the GNU General Public License (GNU GPL) and GNU Lesser General Public License (GNU LGPL), and is a key component of the GNU toolchain. It is the standard compiler for the free software Unix-like operating systems and Apple Mac OS X.

Originally named the GNU C Compiler, because it only handled the C programming language, GCC 1.0 was released in 1987, and the compiler was extended to compile C++ in December of that year. Front-ends were later developed for Fortran, Pascal, Objective-C, Java, and Ada, among others.

Overview

GCC was started by Richard Stallman in 1985. He extended an existing compiler to compile C. The compiler originally compiled Pastel, an extended, non-portable dialect of Pascal, and was written in Pastel. It was rewritten in C by Len Tower and Stallman, and released in 1987 as the compiler for the GNU Project, in order to have a compiler available that was free software. Its development was supervised by the Free Software Foundation.

In 1997, a group of developers, dissatisfied with the slow pace and closed nature of official GCC development, formed a project called EGCS (Experimental/Enhanced GNU Compiler System), which merged several experimental forks into a single project forked from GCC. EGCS development subsequently proved more vigorous than GCC development, and EGCS was eventually "blessed" as the official version of GCC in April 1999.

GCC is now maintained by a varied group of programmers from around the world. It has been ported to more kinds of processors and operating systems than any other compiler.

As well as being the official compiler of the GNU system, including Linux-based variants (GNU/Linux), GCC has been adopted as the main compiler used to build and develop other operating systems, including the BSDs, Mac OS X, NeXTSTEP, and BeOS.

In addition to its use in free software, GCC is widely deployed as a tool in commercial and closed-development environments. GCC is also used in popular embedded platforms like Symbian and Playstation.

GCC is often the compiler of choice for developing software that is required to execute on a plethora of hardware. Differences in native compilers lead to difficulties in developing code that will compile correctly on all the compilers and build scripts that will run for all the platforms. By using GCC, the same parser is used for all platforms, so if the code compiles on one, chances are high that it compiles on all.

Languages

The standard compiler release 4.2 includes front-ends for: C, C++ (G++), Java (GCJ), Ada (GNAT), Objective-C, Objective-C++, and Fortran (GFortran). Also available, but not in standard are: Modula-2, Modula-3, Pascal, PL/I, D, Mercury, VHDL.

The Fortran front-end was g77 before version 4.0, which only supports Fortran 77. In newer versions, g77 was dropped in favour of the new GFortran front-end that supports Fortran 95. A front-end for CHILL was previously included, but has been dropped owing to a lack of maintenance.

Architectures

GCC target processors as of version 4.1 include:

• Alpha	• HC12	• IA-64	• PA-RISC	• System/390/ zSeries	• VAX
• ARM	• H8/300	• MorphoSys	• PDP-11	• SuperH	
• Atmel AVR	• IA-32 (x86)	• Motorola 68000	• PowerPC	• SPARC	
• Blackfin	• x86-64	• MIPS	• R8C/M16C/ M32C		

Lesser-known target processors supported in the standard release have included:

• A29K	• D30V	• Intel i960	• MCORE	• Motorola 88000	• V850
• ARC	• DSP16xx	• IP2000	• MMIX	• NS32K	• Xtensa
• C4x	• FR-30	• M32R	• MN10200	• ROMP	
• ETRAX CRIS	• FR-V	• 68HC11	• MN10300	• Stormy16	

Additional processors have been supported by GCC versions maintained separately from the FSF version:

• D10V	• MicroBlaze	• Nios II and Nios	• PDP-10	• MSP430	• Z8000

When retargeting GCC to a new platform, bootstrapping is often used.

Structure

GCC's external interface is generally standard for a Unix compiler. Users invoke a driver program named GCC, which interprets command arguments, decides which language compilers to use for each input file, runs the assembler on their output, and then possibly runs the linker to produce a complete executable binary.

Each of the language compilers is a separate program that takes in source code and produces assembly language. All have a common internal structure. A per-language front-end parser the source code in that language and produces an abstract syntax tree ("tree" for short), and a back-end converts the trees to GCC's Register Transfer Language (RTL). Compiler optimisations and static code analysis techniques (such as FORTIFY_SOURCE, a compiler directive which attempts to discover some buffer overflows) are applied to the code. Finally, assembly language is produced using architecture-specific pattern matching.

Nearly all of GCC is written in C with the exception of the Ada front-end; much of the Ada front-end is written in Ada.

Front-ends

Front-ends vary internally, having to produce trees that can be handled by the back-end. The parsers are hand-coded recursive descent parsers.

Until recently, the tree representation of the program was not fully independent of the processor being targeted. Confusingly, the meaning of a tree was somewhat different for different language front-ends, and front-ends could provide their own tree codes.

In 2005, two new forms of language-independent trees were introduced. These new tree formats are called GENERIC and GIMPLE. Parsing is now done by creating temporary language-dependent trees, and converting them to GENERIC. The so-called "gimplifier" then lowers this more complex form into the simpler SSA-based GIMPLE form which is the common language for a large number of new powerful language-independent and architecture-independent global (function scope) optimisations.

Middle-end

Optimisation on trees does not generally fit into what most compiler developers would consider a front-end task, as it is not language-dependent and does not involve parsing. GCC developers have given this part of the compiler the somewhat contradictory name the "middle-end". These optimisations include dead code elimination, partial redundancy elimination, global value numbering, sparse conditional constant propagation, and scalar replacement of aggregates. Array dependence-based optimisations such as automatic vectorisation are currently being developed.

Back-end

The behaviour of the GCC back-end is partly specified by pre-processor macros and functions specific to a target architecture. For instance to define the endianness, word size, and calling conventions. The front part of the back-end uses these to help decide RTL generation, so although GCC's RTL is nominally processor-independent, the initial sequence of abstract instructions is already adapted to the target.

The exact set of GCC optimisations varies from release-to-release as it develops, but includes the standard algorithms, such as loop optimisation, jump threading, common sub-expression elimination, instruction scheduling, and so forth. The RTL optimisations are of less importance with the recent addition of global SSA-based optimisations on GIMPLE trees, as RTL optimisations have a much more limited scope, and have less high-level information.

A "reloading" phase changes abstract (pseudo-) registers Into real machine registers, using data collected from the patterns describing the target's instruction set. This is a somewhat complicated phase, because it must account for the vagaries of all of GCC's targets.

The final phase is somewhat anticlimaxtic, since the patterns to match were generally chosen during reloading, and so the assembly code is simply built by running substitutions of registers and addresses into the strings specifying the instructions.

Debugging GCC programs

The primary tool for debugging GCC code is the GNU Debugger (gdb). Among more specialised tools are Valgrind for finding memory errors and leaks. The GNU Profiler (gprof) can be used to find out how much time is spent in which routines, and how often they are called; this requires compiling programs with special profiling options.

5.4.3: Intel C++ Compiler

Intel C++ Compiler (also known as icc or icl) describes a group of C/C++ compilers from Intel. Compilers are available for Linux, Microsoft Windows and Mac OS X.

Intel supports compilation for its IA-32, Intel 64, Itanium 2, and XScale processors. The Intel C++ Compiler for x86 and Intel 64 features an automatic vectoriser that can generate SSE, SSE2, and SSE3 SIMD instructions, the embedded variant for Intel Wireless MMX and MMX 2. Since its introduction, the Intel C++ Compiler for IA-32 has greatly increased adoption of SSE2 in Windows application development.

Intel C++ Compiler further supports both OpenMP and automatic parallelisation for symmetric multi-processing. With the add-on product Cluster OpenMP, the compiler can also automatically generate Message Passing Interface calls for distributed memory multi-processing from OpenMP directives (similar to RWCP Omni).

Intel C++ Compiler belongs to the family of compilers with the Edison Design Group front-end (like the SGI MIPSpro, Comeau C++, Portland Group, and others). The compiler is also notable for being widely used for SPEC CPU Benchmarks of IA-32, x86-64, and Itanium 2 architectures.

Optimisations

Intel tunes its compilers to optimise for its hardware platforms to minimise stalls and to produce code that executes in the smallest number of cycles. The Intel C++ Compiler supports three separate high-level techniques for optimising the compiled program Interprocedural Optimisation (IPO), Profile-Guided Optimisation (PGO), and High Level Optimisations (HLO).

Profile-Guided Optimisation refers to a mode of optimisation where the compiler is able to access data from a sample run of the program across a representative input set. The data would indicate which areas of the program are executed more frequently, and which areas are executed less frequently. All optimisations benefit from profile-guided feedback because they are less reliant on heuristics when making compilation decisions.

High Level Optimisations are optimisations performed on a version of the program that more closely represents the source code. High level optimisations include loop interchange, loop fusion, loop unrolling, loop distribution, data prefetch, and more. High level optimisations are usually very aggressive and may take considerable compilation time.

Interprocedural Optimisation applies typical compiler optimisations (such as constant propagation) but using a broader scope that may include multiple procedures, multiple files, or the entire program.

Languages

Intel's suite of compilers has front-ends for C, C++, and for Fortran.

Early versions of Intel C++ Compiler for Linux that pre-date GCC 3.x uses the Dinkumware name mangling scheme in order to provide a more standard implementation of C++ than GCC 2.x, however also making it ABI incompatible with both GCC versions.

Architectures

- IA-32
- x86-64 (Intel 64 and AMD64)
- IA-64 i.e., the "Itanium"
- XScale

Structure

Like many modern optimising compilers, the Intel compiler has a frontend, an optimising middle, and code-generating back-ends.

Flags and Manuals

Windows	Linux	Comment
/Od	-O0	No optimisation. Useful if you want a quick compile.
/O1	-O1	Optimise for size
/O2	-O2	Optimise for speed and enable some optimisation
/O3	-O3	Enable all optimisations as O2, and intensive loop optimisations
/fast ipo -	-fast	Shorthand. On windows equates to "/O3 /Qipo" on Linux "-O3 - static". Useful if you want to compile your program for release.
/Qprof_gen	-prof_gen	Compile the program and instrument it for a profile generating run.
/Qprof_use	-prof_use	May only be used after running a program that was previously compiled using prof_gen. Uses profile information during each step of the compilation process.

Debugging

The Intel compiler provides debugging information that is standard for the common debuggers (DWARF 2 on Linux, similar to gdb, and COFF for Windows). The flags to compile with debugging information are /Zi on Windows and -g on Linux.

Intel also provides its own debugger called idb, which can be run in both dbx and gdb compatible command mode.

While the Intel compiler can generate a gprof compatible profiling output, Intel also provides a kernel level, system-wide statistical profiler as a separate product called VTune. VTune features an easy-to-use GUI (integrated into Visual Studio for Windows, Eclipse for Linux) as well as a command line interface.

5.4.4: Local C Compiler

LCC ("Local C Compiler" or "Little C Compiler") is a small free retargetable compiler program for the ANSI C programming language. It was developed by Chris Fraser and David Hanson. ID Software's computer game Quake III relies on a modified version of LCC to compile source code for its virtual machine.

LCC

LCC can generate code for several processor architectures, including Alpha, SPARC, MIPS, and x86 (PCs); there is also an LCC back-end that generates MSIL.

LCC-win32

The **LCC-win32** or **LCCWin32** system is a full featured C Development Environment for the Microsoft Windows operating system.

It features:

- Compiler
- Linker
- IDE with integrated resource editor
- Diverse utilities like a profiler, browser, function call browser, revision control system and a lot more.

5.4.5: Watcom C Compiler

The Watcom C/C++ Compiler is esteemed amongst DOS developers by the high execution speed of the compiled code it produces and for having been one of the first compilers to support the Intel 80386 "protected mode". In the mid-1990s, some of the most technically ambitious DOS games such as Doom and Duke Nukem 3D were built using Watcom C.

Though no longer sold commercially by Sybase, the Watcom C/C++ Compiler and the Watcom Fortran compiler have been made available as the open source Open Watcom package with the assistance of SciTech Software. The code is portable, and like many other open source compiler projects such as GCC, the compiler back-end (code generator) is retargetable. The compiler can be operated from, and generate executable code for, the DOS, OS/2 and Windows operating systems. It also supports NLM targets for Novell NetWare. There is ongoing work to retarget it for the Linux and modern BSD (e.g., FreeBSD) operating systems, running on x86, PowerPC and other processors. The Open Watcom C/C++ version 1.4 release on December 2005 has Linux x86 as an experimental target, supported from NT or OS/2 host platforms. There is code for an abandoned QNX version, but libraries necessary for it to be compiled could not be released as open source.

5.4.6: TenDRA Compiler

The **TenDRA Compiler** is a C/C++ Compiler for POSIX compatible operating systems available under the terms of the BSD license.

It was originally developed by the Defence Evaluation and Research Agency (DERA) in the United Kingdom. It has been offered as a BSD-licensed open source project through the website tendra.org.

Now the TenDRA split into 2 projects, TenDRA.org and Ten15.org

The goals of *TenDRA.org* are:

- to produce correct code continuously,
- to ensure code correctness through various means,
- to improve the performance of the compiler and resulting code continuously, unless it would jeopardise the points above.

The goals of *Ten15.org* are:

- to produce correct code continuously,
- to improve the performance of the compiler and resulting code continuously, unless it would jeopardise the point above,
- to create tools that facilitate programming, not to have programming that facilitates the tools,
- to be a friendly competitor to GCC in order to get a best-of-breed compiler.

Features of both compilers include good standards compliance and a smaller code size than the same programs compiled on GCC. C++ support is not as developed as C support, but an STL supporting release is expected soon. TenDRA uses the Architecture Neutral Distribution Format (ANDF), a specification created by the Open Group, as its Intermediate language.

There have been efforts to port the FreeBSD kernel to this compiler.

5.4.7: Tiny C Compiler

The **Tiny C Compiler** (aka TCC, tcc, or TinyCC) is an x86 C language compiler created by Fabrice Bellard. It is designed to work for slow computers with little disk space (e.g., on rescue disks). It can be used on MS Windows operating system too. TCC is distributed under the GNU Lesser General Public License (LGPL).

TCC supports much of ANSI C, much of the new ISO C99 standard and many GNUC extensions including inline assembly. However, it does make some compromises, and improving TCC to achieve compliance might significantly slow it down. Examples of unsupported areas are trigraph handling, proper type and expression checking, and incorrect nested macro expansion.

Features

TCC has the following features:

- Small-can compile and execute C code everywhere, for example on rescue disks (about 100KB for x86 TCC executable, including C pre-processor, C compiler, assembler and linker).
- Fast-tcc generates optimised x86 code. No byte code overhead. It compiles, assembles and links about 9 times faster than GCC.
- Any C dynamic library can be used directly. TCC is heading towards full ISOC99 compliance. TCC can of course compile itself.
- Includes an optional memory and bound checker. Bound-checked code can be mixed freely with standard code.
- Compile and execute C source directly. No linking or assembly necessary. Full C pre-processor and GNU-like assembler included.
- C script is supported: just add '#!/usr/local/bin/tcc -run' at the first line of your C source, and execute it directly from the command line.
- With libtcc, you can use TCC as a back-end for dynamic code generation.
- Few dependencies. It includes its own handwritten lexer, and it is implemented using a recursive descent parser. Thus, building TCC requires few other libraries.

Its LGPL license permits anyone to use, modify, and/or redistribute the software, and it can be used to develop either open source or proprietary software.

Compiled program performance

Although the TCC compiler itself is exceptionally fast and produces very small executables, there is an inherent trade-off between this size of the compiler and the performance of the code that TCC produces.

TCC does perform a few optimisations, such as constant propagation for all operations, multiplications and divisions are optimised to shifts when appropriate, and comparison operators are specially optimised (by maintaining a special cache for the processor flags). It also does some simple register allocation, which prevents many extraneous save/load pairs inside a single statement.

But in general, TCC's implementation emphasises smallness instead of optimally-performing results. TCC generates code in a single pass, and does not perform most of the optimisations performed by other compilers such as GCC. TCC compiles every statement on its own, and at the end of each statement register values are written back to the stack and must be re-read even if the next line uses the values in registers (creating extraneous save/load pairs between statements). TCC uses only some of the available registers (e.g., on x86 it never uses ebx, esi, or edi because they need to be preserved across function calls).

Here are two benchmark examples:

- Rough benchmarks of a recursive Fibonacci algorithm on a 1.8Ghz Intel Centrino laptop with 512MB RAM yields a noticeable difference in results between Microsoft Visual C++ Compiler 13.10.3052 and TCC. To calculate the 49th Fibonacci number, it took a TCC-compiled program approximately 110 seconds, whereas the same program compiled by VC++ took approximately 93 seconds. Here, TCC takes 18% longer.
- With a TCC modified to compile GCC, running cc1 (the GCC C compiler) on itself required 518 seconds when compiled using GCC 3.4.2 (-O1), 558 seconds using GCC 2.95.3 (-O1), 545 using Microsoft C compiler, and 1145 seconds using TCC. In this case TCC generates code that runs about 100% longer (double the time) of the speed of the other compilers when they are mildly optimising (-O1).

Uses

Well Known uses of TCC include:

- TCCBOOT, an impressive hack where TCC loads and boots a Linux kernel from source in about 10 seconds. That is to say, it is a "boot loader" which reads Linux kernel source code from disk, writes executable instructions to memory, and begins running it. This did require changes to the Linux build process.
- TCC was used to demonstrate a defense against the trusting trust attack.
- TCC has been used to compile GCC, though various patches were required to make this work.
- Cinpy is a Python library that allows you to implement functions with C in Python modules. The functions are compiled with TCC (Tiny C Compiler) in runtime. The results are made callable in Python through the ctypes library.

5.4.8: Microsoft Visual Studio

Microsoft Visual Studio is Microsoft's flagship software development product for computer programmers. It centres on an integrated development environment which lets programmers create stand-alone applications, websites, web applications, and web services that run on any platforms supported by Microsofts. NET Framework (for all versions after 6). Supported platforms include Microsoft Windows servers and workstations, PocketPC, Smartphones, and World Wide Web browsers.

Visual Studio includes the following:

- Visual Basic (.NET)
- Visual C++
- Visual C#
- Visual J#
- ASP.NET

Express editions of Visual Studio have been released by Microsoft for lightweight streamlined development and novice developers. **The Express Editions include:**

- Visual Basic (.NET) 2005 Express Edition
- Visual C# 2005 Express Edition
- Visual C++ 2005 Express Edition
- Visual J# 2005 Express Edition
- Visual Web Developer 2005 Express Edition

Some versions include a developer edition of Microsoft SQL Server. There is also a SQL Server 2005 Express Edition.

In the past, the following products were included:

- Visual InterDev, a web page development application used for modifying Active Server Pages as well as HTML and other web scripting files.
- Visual J++, a Java development tool.
- Visual FoxPro, an xBase programming language now allied to but independent from the Visual Studio platform.
- Visual SourceSafe, a source control application-oriented towards smaller software development projects.

5.4.9: IBM VisualAge

VisualAge was the name of a family of computer-integrated development environments from IBM, which included support for a few popular computer programming languages.

Early History

VisualAge was born in the IBM development lab in Cary, North Carolina. The Cary lab was established in 1984 and staffed at the time primarily with IBM employees transferred from Poughkeepsie, New York. The Lab had responsibility for application development tools. The EZ View dialog manager product, a personal computer derivative of the user interface elements of the ISPF 327x product was one of the products. The Lab also had a group which was one of the early adopters of object-oriented programming technologies within IBM using an internally developed language called ClassC to develop applications with more sophisticated graphical user interfaces which were just starting to be widely available.

Eventually, with the availability of usable implementations of Smalltalk in for IBM PC-AT class machines allowed IBM advanced technology projects experiment with Smalltalk. At about the same time, visual interface construction tools were coming up on the radar screens. Smalltalk research projects such as InterCons by David N. Smith of IBM, and Fabrik by a team at Apple led by Dan Ingalls were building interactive graphical applications built from composition of graphical primitives. Higher level construction of user interfaces was evidenced by other tools such as Jean Marie Hulot's interface builder first done in Lisp and then evolved to become the NeXT interface builder tool in NeXTStep which allowed for building user interfaces by WYSIWYG composition of UI widgets which could be "wired" to each other and to application logic written in Objective-C. The original prototype which led to VisualAge was the implementation of an interface builder like tool within the Smalltalk/V development environment. By the time VisualAge was released as a product, much more emphasis was placed on visual construction of application logic as well as of the user interface. This emphasis was in part due to the "positioning" for "strategic" reasons of Smalltalk as a generator rather than a language within IBM's System Application Architecture.

The VisualAge Name

The name VisualAge was the result of a contest between the members of the development team. After the initial release of VisualAge/Smalltalk the name VisualAge became a brand of its own and VisualAges were produced for several different combinations of languages and platforms.

Languages (not every language is available on every platform listed):

- BASIC
- COBOL
- C
- C++
- Fortran
- Java
- Pacbase
- PL/I
- RPG
- TPF
- Smalltalk

Platforms:

- AIX operating system
- OS/2
- i5/OS (Formerly known as OS/400)
- Linux
- Mac OS X
- Microsoft Windows
- z/VM
- z/OS (Formerly known as OS/390, MVS)

Evolution

Most of the members of the VisualAge family were written in Smalltalk no matter which language they supported for development. The IBM implementation of Smalltalk was produced by Object Technology International which was acquired by IBM and run as a wholly-owned subsidiary for several years before being absorbed into the overall IBM organisation.

VisualAge for Java was based on an extended Smalltalk virtual machine which executed both Smalltalk and Java byte codes. Java natives were actually implemented in Smalltalk.

VisualAge Micro Edition, which supported development of embedded Java applications and cross system development, was a reimplementation of the IDE in Java. This version of VisualAge morphed into the Eclipse Framework.

VisualAge is no longer available. Various members of the family have been replaced by products in the WebSphere Studio family of products. The original VisualAge product (VisualAge for Smalltalk) was licensed by IBM to Instantiations, and the current version is called VA Smalltalk. The C, C++ and Fortran compiler on AIX, Linux and z/OS are renamed as XL compiler series.

CHAPTER

6 The C Programming IDEs

6.1: INTRODUCTION

An IDE (Integrated Development Environment) provides an easy-to-use interface for the programmer. It makes all the involved utilities readily available to the programmer.

Generally, a toolkit may include its own IDE as its constituent part.

E.g.,Turbo C/C++ 3.0 , Visual C++ 6.0

But, some toolkits may require a programmer to use a third party IDE.

E.g.,A 'GCC' programmer may use a third party IDE like Eclipse or Netbeans.

6.2: COMPARISON OF C PROGRAMMING IDEs

	Developer	OS	Software License
Anjuta	Naba Kumar (founder) and others	GNU/Linux	GPL
BabyDevelop	Ulrich Gehring (founder) and others	GNU/Linux, Cygwin, Mac OS X	GPL
C++ Builder	CodeGear	Windows	Proprietary
Code::Blocks	Code::Blocks team	GNU/Linux, Windows	GPL
Dev-C++	Bloodshed Software	Windows	GPL
Eclipse CDT	Eclipse Foundation	Cross-platform	EclipsePublic License
GNAT Programming Studio	AdaCore	GNU/Linux, Windows, Solaris	GPL
KDevelop	KDevelop Team	GNU/Linux, Cygwin, other platforms offering X11	GPL
MinGW Developer Studio	Parinya Thipchart	Cross-platform	Unavailable, ClosedSource
NetBeans	Sun Microsystems C/C++ Pack	Cross-platform	CDDL
Pelles	CPelle Orinius	Windows	Proprietary
Turbo	C++Code	GearWindows	Proprietary
Ultimate++	Ultimate++ Team	Cross-platform	most parts BSD
Visual	C++Microsoft	Windows	Proprietary
wxDev-C++	Guru Kathiresan (founder) and others	Windows	GPL
Xcode	AppleMac	OS X	Proprietary

6.3: FEATURES OF C PROGRAMMING IDEs

6.3.1: Anjuta

Anjuta is an integrated development environment for C and C++ on GNU/Linux. It has been written for GTK+/GNOME and features a number of advanced programming facilities. These include project management, application wizards, an interactive debugger built over gdb, and a powerful source code editor with source browsing, code completion and syntax highlighting.

Anjuta is free software distributed under the GNU General Public License (GPL).

Anjuta DevStudio (2.x)

The goal of Anjuta DevStudio is to provide a customisable and extensible IDE framework and at the same time provides the implementations of common development tools. libanjuta is the framework that realises the Anjuta IDE plugin framework and Anjuta DevStudio realises many of the common development plugins.

It integrates many new programming tools such as Glade Interface Designer, Devhelp API help browser, etc.

6.3.2: C++ Builder

Borland C++ Builder, often abbreviated BCB, is a popular rapid application development (RAD) environment produced by the CodeGear subsidiary of Borland for writing programs in the C++ programming language. It closely resembles Delphi, and as a result many consider it to be a C++ version of Delphi. Most components developed in Delphi can be used in C++ Builder with no modification, although the reverse is not true.

C++ Builder includes tools that allow true drag-and-drop visual development, making programming easier by incorporating a WYSIWYG GUI builder into its IDE.

History

C++ Builder originally targeted only the Microsoft Windows platform. Later versions incorporated Borland CLX, a cross-platform development visual component library based on Qt, that supports Windows and Linux.

In 2003 Borland released C++ BuilderX (CBX), which was written using the same framework as JBuilder and bore little resemblance to either C++ Builder or Delphi. This product was aimed at developing large programs for enterprises; however, it did not have commercial success. At the end of 2004 Borland announced that it would continue to develop the classic C++ Builder and bundle it with the Delphi development suite, abandoning C++ BuilderX.

About a year after the announcement, Borland released Borland C++ Builder 2006, providing improved configuration management and bug fixes. C++ Builder 2006 is part of Borland Developer Studio, a single robust package containing Delphi, C++ Builder, and C#Builder. Borland later revived the "Turbo" brand and released two "Turbo" editions of C++ Builder: Turbo C++ Professional, and Turbo C++ Explorer (free).

In 2007 Borland released C++ Builder 2007, providing full API support for Microsoft Vista, increased ANSI C++ Conformance, up to 500 per cent faster in-IDE build performance, support for MSBuild, DBX4 database architecture, and "VCL for the Web" which supports AJAX. The API support for Microsoft Vista includes themed applications and seamless VCL support for Aero and Vista Desktop.

6.3.3: Code::Blocks

Code::Blocks is a free/open source, cross-platform IDE. It is developed in C++ using wxWidgets. Using a plugin architecture, its capabilities and features are defined by the provided plugins. Currently, Code::Blocks is oriented towards C/C++.

Code::Blocks is being developed for Windows and Linux. Users have successfully built Code::Blocks under FreeBSD and (to date still with some UI problems) under Mac OS X.

The development releases after May 23rd, 2007 require wxwidgets2.8.

The old branch 1.0 release ended with the stable release 1.0rc2, October 25, 2005. Development releases, which are usually more stable and functional than 1.0rc2 are slowly working towards release 2.0

Features

Compiler-related features

- Multiple compiler support
  - MinGW / GCC C/C++
  - Digital Mars C/C++
  - Digital Mars D (with limits)
  - SDCC (Small device C compiler)
  - Microsoft Visual C++ Toolkit 2003
  - Microsoft Visual C++ Express 2005 (with limits)
  - Borland C++ 5.5
  - Watcom
  - Intel C++ compiler
  - GNU Fortran
  - GNU ARM
  - GNU GDC
- Multi-target projects
- Workspace support
- Import Dev-C++ projects
- Import MSVC projects and workspaces

Interface features

- Syntax highlighting
- Code folding
- Code completion
- Class browser
- Squirrel scripting engine
- To-do list management with different users
- Devpack support (installation packages for Dev-C++)
- wxSmith plugin (a wxWidgets RAD tool,

6.3.4: Dev-C++

Dev-C++ is a free integrated development environment (IDE) distributed under the GNU General Public License for programming in C/C++. It is bundled with the open source MinGW compiler. The IDE is written in Delphi.

The project is sponsored by SourceForge. Dev-C++ was originally founded by programmer Colin Laplace and his associated company, Bloodshed Software. Dev-C++ currently runs exclusively on Microsoft Windows. At one time, a Linux port was available, but that project has since been abandoned.

The program itself has a look-and-feel similar to that of the more widely-used Microsoft Visual Studio. One additional aspect of Dev-C++ is its use of DevPaks, packaged extensions on the programming environment with additional libraries, templates, and utilities. DevPaks often contain, but are not limited to, GUI utilities, including popular toolkits such as GTK+, wxWidgets, and FLTK. Other DevPaks include libraries for more advanced function use.

6.3.5: DJGPP

DJGPP (DJ's GNU Programming Platform) is a 32-bit C/C++/ObjC/Ada/Fortran development suite for 386+ PCs that runs under DOS (or any OS that runs DOS .EXEs, such as Microsoft Windows or IBM OS/2). It was developed by DJ Delorie, who started the project in 1989. It is a port of the popular GCC compiler, as well as many other GNU utilities such as cp, ls, mv, awk, sed, and ld to DOS DPMI (DOS Protected Mode Interface). It uses a flat memory model, where code and data segments are coincident. Additional segments can be accessed indirectly.

Compatibility

DJGPP presents the programmer an interface which is compatible with the ANSI C and C99 standards, unofficial DOS standards, and the POSIX UNIX standard. Compiled binaries are long file name-aware and handle such file names under Windows 9x+ by default. TSRs to support LFNs under Windows NT 4 or pure DOS are available. Currently, no x86-64 version of Windows supports 16-bit programs (or even programs with 16-bit stubs, like DJGPP) except via emulation.

6.3.6: Windows Ports of the GNU Toolkit

Cygwin: A UNIX compatibility layer with many ported libraries and applications

MinGW: A port of the GNU toolkit for Windows, designed to require minimal runtime support

6.3.7: KDevelop

KDevelop is a free IDE for GNU/Linux and other Unix-like operating systems. KDevelop is licensed under the GPL license.

KDevelop does not include a compiler; instead, it uses the GNU Compiler Collection (or, optionally, another compiler) to produce executable code.

The current version, 3.4, supports many programming languages such as Ada, Bash, C, C++, Fortran, Java, Pascal, Perl, PHP, Python, Ruby, and SQL.

History

KDevelop 3.0 was a complete rewrite of KDevelop 2. It was released together with KDE 3.2 in February 2004.

Features

KDevelop uses an embedded text editor component through KPart technology. The default editor is KDE Advanced Text Editor, which can optionally be replaced with a Qt Designer-based editor. This list focuses on the features of KDevelop itself. For features specific to the editor component, see the article on Kate.

- Source code editor with syntax highlighting and automatic indentation (Kate).
- Project management for different project types, such as Automake, qmake for Qt based projects and Ant for Java based projects.
- Class browser.
- GUI Designer.
- Front-end for the GNU Compiler Collection.
- Front-end for the GNU Debugger.
- Wizards for generating and updating class definitions and application framework.
- Automatic code completion (C/C++).
- Built-in Doxygen support.
- Revision control (also known as SCM) support. Supported systems include CVS, Subversion, Perforce and ClearCase.

KDevelop 3 is a completely plugin-based architecture. When a developer makes a change, he only has to compile the plugin. There is a possibility to keep several profiles each of which determines which plugins to be loaded. KDevelop does not come with a text editor, but instead uses a plugin for this purpose as well. KDevelop is programming language and build system-independent, supporting KDE, GNOME, and many other technologies such as Qt, GTK+, and wxWidgets.

KDevelop has a variety of supported languages, including C, C++, Perl, Python, PHP, Java, Fortran, Ruby, Ada, Pascal, SQL, and Bash scripting. Supported build systems include GNU (automake), cmake, qmake, and make for custom projects (KDevelop does not destroy your own Makefiles if that's what you want to use) and scripting projects which don't need one.

Code *completion* is available for C and C++. Symbols are kept in a Berkeley DB file for quick lookups without re-parsing. KDevelop also offers a developer framework which helps to write new parsers for other programming languages.

An integrated debugger lets you graphically do all the debugging with breakpoints and backtraces. It even works with dynamically loaded plugins unlike command line gdb.

Quick Open allows quick navigation between files.

Currently, 50 to 100 plugins exist for the IDE. Major ones include persistent project-wide code bookmarks, *Code abbreviations* which let you quickly expand text, a *Source formatter* which reformats your code to a *style guide* before it is saved, *Regular expressions search*, and project-wide *search/replace* which helps with refactoring code.

6.3.8: NetBeans

NetBeans refers to both a platform for the development of Java desktop applications, and an integrated development environment (IDE) developed using the NetBeans Platform.

The NetBeans Platform allows applications to be developed from a set of modular software components called modules. A module is a Java archive file that contains Java classes written to interact with the NetBeans Open APIs and a manifest file that identifies it as a module. Applications built on modules can be extended by adding new modules. Since modules can be developed independently, applications based on the NetBeans Platform can be easily and powerfully extended by third party developers.

NetBeans C/C++ Pack:

The NetBeans C/C++ Pack adds support for C/C++ developers to NetBeans IDE 5.5.

This pack lets C/C++ developers use their specified set of compilers and tools in conjunction with NetBeans IDE to build native applications for e.g., MS Windows, Linux, and Solaris. The pack makes the editor language-aware for C/C++, and provides project templates, a dynamic class browser, make file support, and debugger functionality. Developers can also extend the pack wlth their own additional functionalities.

6.3.9: QDevelop

QDevelop is a development environment entirely dedicated to Qt4. QDevelop requires Qt4, GCC under Linux or MinGW under Windows, possibly gdb for program debugging and ctags for code completion. QDevelop is available in English, French, German, Dutch, Polish, Spanish, Chinese, Russian, Italian, Ukrainian, Czech and Portuguese.

QDevelop is not a KDevelop-like or reduced. It is an independent IDE dedicated to Qt and is totally independent of KDevelop. Less complete, but faster, light and especially multi-platform. QDevelop and KDevelop have different code sources.

Features:

- Cross-platform: Supports Linux, Windows 2000/XP/Vista, Mac OS X and FreeBSD
- Reading and writing project files (with some small restrictions)
- Add/Delete and edit project files (or external files)
- Management of normal projects and project subdirectories.
- Independent build for each project. Only modified projects are rebuilt.
- A powerful editor with code completion, syntax highligthing, bookmarks, auto-brackets, auto-indentation, auto-save before build, line numbers and selection margin.

- A class browser which allows the programmer to browse, navigate, or visualise the structure of classes, members and functions.
- Double-click on compilation warnings/errors to open the corresponding editor.
- Debugging with gdb. Toggle breakpoints by click in the line number on editor or by right click. Local variables are automatically displayed when program stops at breakpoint.
- In the editor, F1 calls Assistant to display help for the word under the cursor.
- Open Source
- Freeware

6.3.10: Turbo C++

Turbo C++ is a Borland C++ compiler and Integrated Development Environment (IDE), famous for its high compilation and linkage speed – hence the term "Turbo". It was a part of Borland's highly popular family of compilers including Turbo Pascal, Turbo Basic, Turbo Prolog and Turbo C. Turbo C++ was a successor of Turbo C, expanding the compiler similarly to how Turbo Pascal 5.5 added object functionality to the earlier Turbo Pascal versions. Unlike Turbo Pascal, however, Turbo C++ always adhered to C++ language standards of its time. The MS-DOS product was never capable of compiling ISO-standard C++, however, because development on it was discontinued before the standard was completed.

Borland has recently brought back the "Turbo" product-line with all-new versions of Turbo C++, Turbo Delphi (including a special .Net compatible version), and Turbo C# for Win32 and .NET programming.

Version History

The first release of Turbo C++ was made available during the MS-DOS reign on personal computers. It came up in versions 1.0, running on OS/2 and version 1.01, released on February 28, 1991, running on MS-DOS. The latter was able to generate both COM and EXE programs, and was shipped with Borland's Turbo Assembler compiler for Intel x86 processors. The initial version of the Turbo C++ compiler was based on a front-end developed by TauMetric (TauMetric was later acquired by Sun Microsystems and their front-end was incorporated in Sun C++ 4.0, which shipped in 1994). This compiler supported the AT and T 2.0 release of C++.

Turbo C++ 3.0 was released in 1991 (shipping on November 20), and came in amidst expectations of the coming release of Turbo C++ for Microsoft Windows. Turbo C++ v3.0 first came as an MS-DOS compiler, supporting C++ templates, generation of DOS and protected mode executables, as well as generation of code, targeting specific legacy CPUs such as Intel 80186. The language implementation was updated to the latest AT&T release of C++.

After Windows 3.0 became available, Turbo C++ was sold with MS-Windows support. First Windows-based IDE was Turbo C++ 3.0 for Windows, followed by Turbo C++ 3.1 and Turbo C++ 4.5. It is possible that the jump from version 1.x to version 3.x was in part an attempt to link Turbo C++ release numbers with Microsoft Windows versions; however, it seems more likely that this jump was simply to synchronise Turbo C and Turbo C++, since Turbo C 2.0 (1989) and Turbo C++ 1.0 (1990) had come out roughly at the same time, and the next generation 3.0 was a merger of both the C and C++ compilers.

With version 3.0, Borland introduced a distinction between "Turbo C++" and "Borland C++". The former was marketed as a somewhat low-end product, while the latter was geared towards professional applications (it included additional tools and a stronger optimiser).

Version 4.0 was released in November 1993 and was notable (among other things) for its robust support of templates. In particular, it was instrumental in the development of the Standard Template Library, expression templates, and the first advanced applications of template metaprogramming. With the success of Delphi, Borland ceased work on their Borland C++ Suite and concentrated on C++ Builder for Windows, which used the same rapid application framework as Delphi but largely the same back-end compiler technology, and that change in emphasis led to the end of active development on Borland C++/Turbo C++ (until 2006, see below).

Turbo C++ v1.01 for DOS is currently freely distributed by Borland, and can be downloaded from their Antique Software website.

Currently, Borland also offers Borland Turbo C++ 4.5 in a package called Borland Turbo C++ Suite in their shop. This suite categorised in their Classic Products.

Turbo C++ 2006, a subset version of Borland C++ Builder, was released in 2006 and is available in 'Explorer' and 'Professional' editions. The Explorer edition is free to download and distribute while the Professional edition is a commercial product.

6.3.11: Eclipse CDT

C/C++ Development Tools project, commonly known as CDT, this is the most popular project under the auspices of the Eclipse Foundation. It adds C/C++ Project structure and syntax recognition to the Eclipse platform. However, CDT does not include its own set of build tools but uses the GNU tool chain instead (by default). On UNIX-like operating systems, these tools are typically supplied as part of the distribution and might not require the user to perform additional configuration for Eclipse. On Windows, however, users must supply their own build tools. This can be done through a GNU port such as MinGW or cygwin, or possibly by supplying tools from another IDE such as Visual Studio.

6.3.12: IcyOwl

IcyOwl is an Open Source C++ Integrated Development Environment(IDE) distributed under GNU General Public License. It is written in C++ and wxWidgets API. IcyOwl is cross-platform, which means that it runs on many Operating System such as Microsoft Windows and Linux. Mac OS port is still unavailable as of now.

It uses doxygen to generate class tree, but only supports one compiler, that is GCC/ MinGW.

Features:

- Uses MinGW on Windows
- Uses GCC on Linux
- Syntax highlighting
- Code completion
- Class browser
- Project Manager
- Auto generation of Makefile

6.3.13: Ultimate++

Ultimate++ is;

1. A cross-platform graphical widget toolkit for the development of GUI programs.
2. A set of C++ (and U++) libraries (called packages in Ultimate++):
    1. "Core" is the base for all other Ultimate++ libraries.
    2. "CtrlCore" - a base for widgets (or controls).
    3. "CtrlLib" - actual widgets (or controls).
    4. Other libraries (full list available on request from maintainers).
3. An IDE called the IDE.

Those 3 main things together make Ultimate++ an application framework comparable to Java or .Net framework.

6.3.14: Visual C++

Microsoft Visual C++ (also known as MSVC) is an integrated development environment (IDE) product engineered by Microsoft for the C, C++, and C++/CLI programming languages. It has tools for developing and debugging C++ Code, especially that written for the Microsoft Windows API, the DirectX API, and the Microsoft .NET framework.

Features

Visual C++ has features such as syntax highlighting, IntelliSense (a coding autocompletion feature) and advanced debugging functionality. For example, it allows for remote debugging using a separate computer and allows debugging by stepping through code a line at a time. The "edit and continue" functionality allows changing the source code and rebuilding the program during program debugging, without restarting the debugged program.

The compile and build system feature, precompiled header files, "minimal rebuild" functionality and incremental link: these features significantly shorten turn-around time to edit, compile and link the program, especially for large software projects.

History

The predecessor to Visual C++ was called Microsoft C/C++.

- **Visual C++ 1.0**, which included MFC 2.0, was the first version of Visual C++, released in 1992, available in both 16-bit and 32-bit versions.
- **Visual C++ 1.5**, which included MFC 2.5, added OLE 2.0 and ODBC support to MFC. It was 16-bit only and was the first version of Visual C++ that came only on CD-ROM.
- **Visual C++ 1.52c** was a patched version of 1.5, but deserves its own entry since it is the last, and arguably most popular, development platform for Microsoft Windows 3.x. It was available through Microsoft Developer Network until 2003.
- **Visual C++ 2.0**, which included MFC 3.0, was the first version to be 32-bit only. In many ways, this version was ahead of its time because Windows 95, then codenamed "Chicago", was not released, and Windows NT had only a small market share. As a result, this release was almost a "lost generation". Updates available through subscription included version 2.1 and 2.2. Microsoft included and updated Visual C++ 1.5 as part of this release and both 16-bit and 32-bit version of the Control Development Kit (CDK) were included. Visual C++ 2.x also supported Win32s development.
- **Visual C++ 4.0**, which included MFC 4.0, was designed for Windows 95 and Windows NT. Updates available through subscription included Visual C++ 4.1 and Visual C++ 4.2, which no longer supported Win32s.
- **Visual C++ 5.0**, which included MFC 4.2, was a major upgrade from 4.2.
- **Visual C++ 6.0**, which included MFC 4.2, was released in 1998. The release was somewhat controversial since it did not include an expected update to MFC. Visual C++ 6.0 is still quite popular and often used to maintain legacy projects. There are, however, issues with this version under Windows XP, especially under the debugging mode (e.g.,: the values of static variables do not display). The debugging issues can be solved with a patch called the "Visual C++ 6.0 Processor Pack" downloadable from http://msdn2.microsoft.com/en-us/vstudio/aa718349.aspx; curiously, this page stresses that users must also be running Windows 98, Windows NT 4.0, or Windows 2000.
- **Visual C++ .NET 2002** (known also as Visual C++ 7.0), which included MFC 7.0, was released in 2002 with support for link time code generation and debugging runtime checks, .NET 1.0 and Visual C# and managed C++ extensions for .NET. The new user interface used many of the hot keys and conventions of Visual Basic, which accounted from some of its unpopularity among C++ developers.
- **Visual C++ .NET 2003** (known also as Visual C++ 7.1), which included MFC 7.1, was released in 2003 along with .NET 1.1 and was a major upgrade to Visual C++ .NET 2002. It was considered a patch to Visual C++ .NET 2002 and shipped for minimal cost to owners of that version.

- **eMbedded Visual C++** was used to develop for the Windows CE operating system. eMbedded Visual C++ was replaced as a separate development environment by Microsoft Visual Studio 2005.
- **Visual C++ 2005** (known also as Visual C++ 8.0), which included MFC 8.0, was released in November 2005. This version supports .NET 2.0 and dropped managed C++ for C++/CLI. It also introduced OpenMP. With Visual C++ 2005, Microsoft also introduced Team Foundation Server. It is currently the latest stable release.
- **Visual C++ 2008** was previously known by the internal code name of Orcas. In addition to full support for .NET 3.0, it will include many enhancements to C++ development including improved intellisense and updates to MFC.

Visual C++ 2005 Express

This Microsoft Visual C++ (or Visual C++ 8.0) is available in two flavours: as a part of Microsoft Visual Studio 2005, and as a stand-alone "Express Edition" product.

Microsoft Visual C++ 2005 Express Edition is available from the Microsoft Developer Network (MSDN) website as a free download. However, the Visual C++ 2005 SP1 Redistributables are not included and could not be downloaded from Microsoft. As Microsoft says, "Once an application is rebuilt with Visual C++ 2005 Service Pack 1, it will need the Visual C++ 2005 Service Pack 1 version of the Visual C++ libraries during runtime". Thus, an executable compiled using default options (dynamic linking) in Visual C++ 2005 Express SP1 could not be deployed to PCs that do not have Visual C++ 2005 Express SP1 installed.

64-bit

Visual Studio 2005 Standard and Professional editions have x64 compiler support, and Visual Studio 2005 Team System supports IA-64 and x64. Before Visual C++ 2005 was released, programmers were supposed to get the Platform SDK if they wanted to write 64-bit programs. That included the 64-bit compilers and the 64-bit versions of the Visual C++ 6.0 libraries.

6.3.15: Xcode

Xcode is Apple's suite of tools for developing software on Mac OS X. Xcode 2.4.1, the latest version, is bundled free with Mac OS X v10.4, though is not installed by default. It contains "stability, performance, and security enhancements" and is available for free from Apple Developer Connection. Apple has released a beta version of Xcode 3 to developers who are testing the upcoming 10.5 "Leopard" release of the Mac OS X operating system.

When the acronym IDT has been coined, there is no need to repeat/reproduce the expansion, every time. This occurs regularly. The main application of the suite is the integrated development environment (IDE), also named Xcode. The Xcode suite also includes most of Apple's developer documentation, and Interface Builder, an application used to construct graphical interfaces.

The Xcode suite includes a modified version of free software GNU Compiler Collection (GCC, apple-darwin8-gcc,4.0.1), and can compile C, C++, Objective-C, Objective-C++,

Java, and AppleScript, source code with a variety of programming models, including but not limited to Cocoa, Carbon, and Java. Third parties have added support for GNU Pascal, Free Pascal, Ada and Perl. The Xcode suite uses GDB as the back-end for its debugger.

Major Features

Among the highly touted features of the Xcode suite is the technology to distribute the building of source code over multiple computers. Xcode has two systems for distributing compilation. The original system uses the Bonjour protocol and the free software distcc. The more recently added system, called *Dedicated Network Builds*, scales better to larger configurations than distcc but does not support Bonjour's auto-discovery service.

Due to modifications to GCC by Apple, Xcode can build universal binaries which allows software to run on both PowerPC and Intel-based (x86) platforms. Furthermore, the modified GCC can build 32- and 64-bit applications for both architectures.

Xcode also includes Apple's WebObjects tools and frameworks for building Java web applications and web services (previously sold as a separate $699 product).

In August 2006, Apple announced that DTrace, a dynamic tracing framework created by Sun Microsystems and released as part of OpenSolaris, would be integrated into Xcode.

History

The Xcode suite, like Mac OS X itself, had its roots in technology from NeXT. Prior to the October 24, 2003 release of Mac OS X v10.3, Apple referred to the suite of tools as Developer Tools. The Xcode IDE was developed from and superseded Apple's earlier IDE, Project Builder.

SECTION

SECTION-IV: C PROGRAMMING IN DIFFERENT ENVIRONMENTS

Objectives

C language is available on all the platforms. A platform is a combination of the underlying processor and the operating system. As a programmer one needs to worry only about the operating system factor. The respective toolkit available for that operating system takes care of the underlying processor. The most common operating systems confronted by today's programmers are Windows and Linux. Generally, they confront DOS during their academic tenure. Applying the knowledge of C language on different operating systems requires a programmer to learn appropriate toolkits and IDEs available on those systems. This section briefly discusses C programming under DOS, Windows and Linux environments. It follows a case study-based approach for the sake of brevity.

Contents:

CHAPTER

7 C Programming in DOS Environment

7.1: Assumptions

7.2: Set the PATH Environment Variable

7.3: Open Turbo C/C++ 3.0 IDE

7.4: Set the Directories for the IDE

7.5: Create the Source Code Files

7.6: Convert the Source Code into an Executable File

7.7: Test Run the Executable from the IDE

7.8: Location of the Executable

Turbo C/C++ 3.0 (TC) is the commonly used C programming toolkit in DOS environment. We will develop a very simple program in C language using the 'Turbo C/C++ 3.0' (TC) toolkit in DOS environment.

7.1: ASSUMPTIONS

'D:\TC' directory contains the TC installation.

'D:\cprogs' directory contains the C source code files.

7.2: SET THE PATH ENVIRONMENT VARIABLE

Set the operating systems PATH environment variable to include the Turbo C/C++ 3.0 toolkit in it. Type the following DOS command at the command prompt to set the PATH.

```
D:\>PATH=%PATH%;D:\TC\BIN
```

7.3: OPEN TURBO C/C++ 3.0 IDE

Type the following DOS command at the command prompt to open the Turbo C/C++ 3.0 IDE.

```
D:\>tc
```

7.4: SET THE DIRECTORIES FOR THE IDE

In Turbo C/C++ IDE select the following menu to open the 'Directories' dialog box to set the IDE's directory variables:

Options ? Directories ...

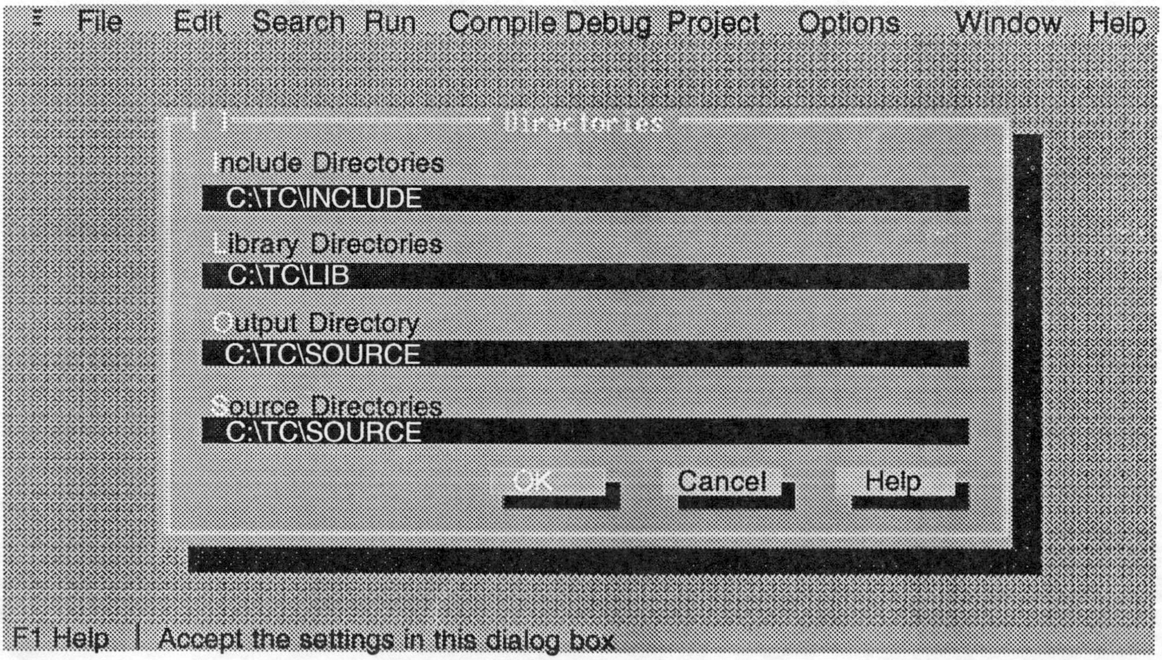

7.5: CREATE THE SOURCE CODE FILES

This program uses two source files;

our_include.h : which defines two constants A and B

add.c : which adds them and displays the result.

```
/* our_include.h */
#define A 10
#define B 20

/* add.c */
#include "our_include.h"
main()
{
        int C;
        C = A + B;
        printf("%d\n", C);
}
```

7.6: CONVERT THE SOURCE CODE INTO AN EXECUTABLE FILE

In Turbo C/C++ IDE select the following menu to create the corresponding executable:

Compile ⟶ Make

7.7: TEST RUN THE EXECUTABLE FROM THE IDE

In Turbo C/C++ IDE select the following menu to test run the corresponding executable:

Run ⟶ Run

7.8: LOCATION OF THE EXECUTABLE

The corresponding executable file (add.exe) will be present in the 'D:\cprogs' directory. Now you can directly run the program by executing the 'add.exe' file from its location.

CHAPTER

8 C Programming in Windows Environment

Visual C++ is the commonly used C programming toolkit in Windows environment.

We will develop a very simple program in C language using the 'Visual C++ 6.0' toolkit in Windows environment.

8.1: OPEN THE VISUAL C++ 6.0 IDE

Open the Visual C++ 6.0 IDE from the Start menu.

Start → Programs → Microsoft Visual Studio 6.0 → Microsoft Visual C++ 6.0

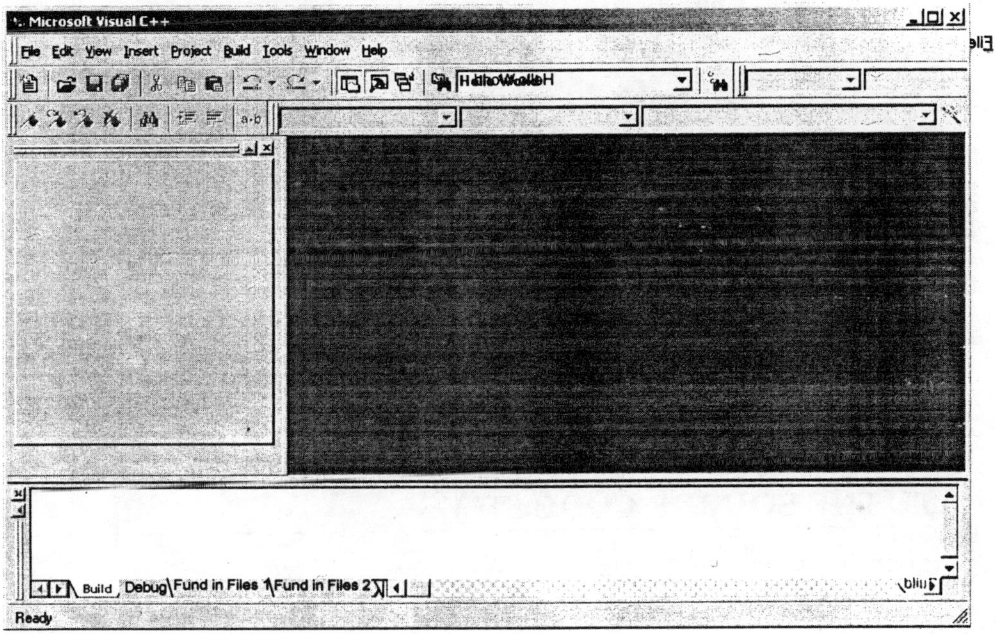

8.2: CREATE A PROJECT

The Microsoft Visual C++ toolkit expects a project for every application. Create a project using the following menu options from the IDE:

File → New → Projects

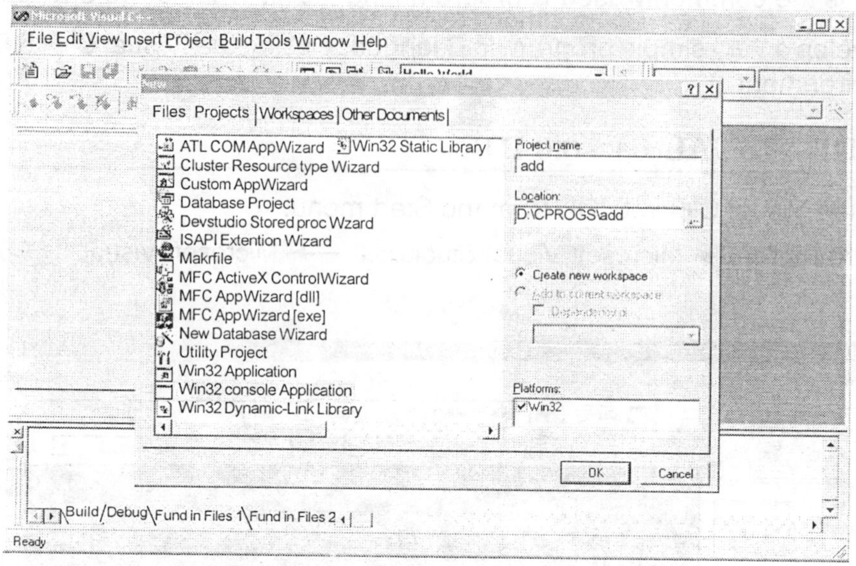

Settings for the project:

Project Type: Win32 Console Application

Project Name: add

Location: D:\cprogs\add

8.3: CREATE THE SOURCE CODE FILES

This program uses two source files;

our_include.h : which defines two constants A and B

add.c : which adds them and displays the result.

Add a header file (our_include.h) to the project through the following menu:

File ⟶ New ⟶ Files ⟶ C/C++ Header File

```
/* our_include.h */
#define A 10
#define B 20
```

Add a C source file (add.c) to the project through the following menu:

File ⟶ New ⟶ Files ⟶ C++ Source File

```
/* add.c */
#include "our_include.h"
main()
{
    int C;
    C = A + B;
    printf("%d\n", C);
}
```

8.4: CONVERT THE SOURCE CODE INTO AN EXECUTABLE FILE

In Visual C++ 6.0 IDE select the following menu to create the corresponding executable:

Build ⟶ Build add.exe

8.5: TEST RUN THE EXECUTABLE FROM THE IDE

In Visual C++ 6.0 IDE select the following menu to test run the corresponding executable:

Build ⟶ Execute add.exe

8.6: LOCATION OF THE EXECUTABLE

In Debug build, the corresponding executable file (add.exe) will be present in the 'D:\cprogs\add\Debug' directory. Now you can directly run the program by executing the 'add.exe' file from its location.

In Release build, the corresponding executable file (add.exe) will be present in the 'D:\cprogs\add\Release' directory. Now you can directly run the program by executing the 'add.exe' file from its location.

END

CHAPTER

9 C Programming in Linux Environment

GNU C Compiler (GCC) toolkit is commonly used in Linux environment. We will develop a very simple program in C language using the 'GCC' toolkit in Linux environment.

9.1: CREATE THE SOURCE CODE FILES

This program uses two source files; *our_include.h,* which defines two constants A and B, and add.c, which adds them and displays the result. Create the source code files using a text editor (e.g., vi, emacs).

```
$ls
 add.c     our_include.h
$
$cat our_include.h
 #define A 10
 #define B 20
$
$cat add.c
 #include "our_include.h"
 main()
 {
      int C;
      C = A + B;
      printf("%d\n", C);
 }
$
```

(There is no need to include *stdio.h* while using GCC, it is thereby default.)

9.2: CONVERT THE SOURCE CODE INTO AN EXECUTABLE FILE

The 'GCC' program called with option '-o' stores the resultant executable code under the specified filename, here in 'add'. If not specified then a.out is the default output filename.

```
$gcc add.c -o add
$ls
 add add.c our_include.h
$
$./add
 30
$
```

9.3: RUN THE EXECUTABLE

The corresponding executable file 'add' will be present in the same directory. You can execute the same using the following command:

```
$./add
        30
        $
```

SECTION

V: C THROUGH QUESTIONS

Objectives

Converting the theoretical knowledge about C language into a skill-set is a tricky scenario. The professional C programmers need the proficiency to process a C program in the brain. They have to think as if they are the language processors and visualise the entire processing path. This gives them insight for the C language. Reading and mentally processing a C program helps to develop this skill-set. This section gives ample opportunity for the reader for the same. The questions listed down in this section are representative of their multiple possible variants. Each listed question is followed by its answer and brief explanation. A reader is suggested to perform mental-processing on the problem first and then compare the answer. Then compare your understanding with the noted explanation. Here, the process of mental-processing is more important to develop the professional skill-set of a C programmer.

Contents:

C Through Questions

Predict the output or error(s) for the following code snippets:

```
1. void main()
   {
           int const * p=5;
           printf("%d",++(*p));
   }
```

Answer:

Compiler error: Cannot modify a constant value.

Explanation:

p is a pointer to a "constant integer". But we tried to change the value of the "constant integer".

```
2. main()
   {
        char s[ ]="man";
        int i;
        for(i=0;s[ i ];i++)
        printf("\n%c%c%c%c",s[ i ],*(s+i),*(i+s),i[s]);
   }
```

Answer:

```
mmmm
aaaa
nnnn
```

Explanation:

s[i], *(i+s), *(s+i), i[s] are all different ways of expressing the same idea. Generally, array name is the base address for that array. Here, s is the base address. i is the index number/ displacement from the base address. So, indirecting it with * is same as s[i]. i[s] may be surprising. But in the case of c it is same as s[i].

```
3. main()
   {
        float me = 1.1;
        double you = 1.1;
        if(me==you)
        printf("I love U");

     else
              printf("I hate U");
     }
```

Answer:

I hate U

Explanation:

For floating point numbers (float, double, long double) the values cannot be predicted exactly. Depending on the number of bytes, the precision with of the value represented varies. Float takes 4 bytes and long double takes 10 bytes. So, float stores 0.9 with less precision than long double.

Rule of Thumb:

Never compare or at least be cautious when using floating point numbers with relational operators (== , >, <, <=, >=,!=) .

```
4. main()
   {
        static int var = 5;
        printf("%d ",var--);
        if(var)
                main();
   }
```

Answer:

5 4 3 2 1

Explanation:

When static storage class is given, it is initialised once. The change in the value of a static variable is retained even between the function calls. Main is also treated like any other ordinary function, which can be called recursively.

5. main()

```
{
     int c[ ]={2.8,3.4,4,6.7,5};
     int j,*p=c,*q=c;
     for(j=0;j<5;j++) {
          printf(" %d ",*c);
          ++q;     }
     for(j=0;j<5;j++){
          printf(" %d ",*p);
          ++p;     }
}
```

Answer:

2 2 2 2 2 2 3 4 6 5

Explanation:

Initially, pointer c is assigned to both p and q. In the first loop, since only q is incremented and not c , the value 2 will be printed 5 times. In second loop p itself is incremented. So, the values 2 3 4 6 5 will be printed.

6. main()

```
{
     extern int i;
     i=20;
     printf("%d",i);
}
```

Answer:

Linker Error : Undefined symbol '_i'

Explanation:

extern storage class in the following declaration,

extern int i;

specifies to the compiler that the memory for i is allocated in some other program and that address will be given to the current program at the time of linking. But linker finds that no other variable of name i is available in any other program with memory space allocated for it. Hence, a linker error has occurred.

7. main()

```
{
    int i=-1,j=-1,k=0,l=2,m;
   m=i++&&j++&&k++||l++;
    printf("%d %d %d %d %d",i,j,k,l,m);
}
```

Answer:

0 0 1 3 1

Explanation:

Logical operations always give a result of 1 or 0. And also the logical AND (&&) operator has higher priority over the logical OR (||) operator. So, the expression 'i++ && j++ && k++' is executed first. The result of this expression is 0 (-1 && -1 && 0 = 0). Now the expression is 0 || 2 which evaluates to 1 (because OR operator always gives 1 except for '0 || 0' combination – for which it gives 0). So, the value of m is 1. The values of other variables are also incremented by 1.

8. main()

```
{
    char *p;
    printf("%d %d ",sizeof(*p),sizeof(p));
}
```

Answer:

1 2

Explanation:

The sizeof() operator gives the number of bytes taken by its operand. P is a character pointer, which needs one byte for storing its value (a character). Hence, sizeof(*p) gives a value of 1. Since it needs two bytes to store the address of the character pointer sizeof(p) gives 2.

```
9. main()
   {
       int i=3;
       switch(i)
       {
          default:printf("zero");
          case 1: printf("one");
                  break;
         case 2:printf("two");
                 break;
        case 3: printf("three");
                 break;
       }
   }
```

Answer:

three

Explanation:

The default case can be placed anywhere inside the loop. It is executed only when all other cases doesn't match.

```
10. main()
    {
         printf("%x",-1<<4);
    }
```

Answer:

fff0

-1 is internally represented as all 1's. When left shifted four times, the least significant 4 bits are filled with 0's.The %x format specifier specifies that the integer value be printed as a hexadecimal value.

11. main()

```
{
    char string[]="Hello World";
    display(string);
}
    void display(char *string)
{
    printf("%s",string);
}
```

Answer:

Compiler Error : Type mismatch in redeclaration of function display

Explanation:

In the third line, when the function display is encountered, the compiler doesn't know anything about the function display. It assumes the arguments and return types to be integers, (which is the default type). When it sees the actual function display, the arguments and type contradicts with what it has assumed previously. Hence, a compile time error occurs.

12. main()

```
{
    int c=- -2;
    printf("c=%d",c);
}
```

Answer:

c=2;

Explanation:

Here unary minus (or negation) operator is used twice. Same maths rules applies, i.e., minus * minus= plus.

Note:

However, you cannot give like --2. Because -- operator can only be applied to variables as a decrement operator (e.g., i--). 2 is a constant and not a variable.

13.
```
#define int char
main()
{
    int i=65;
    printf("sizeof(i)=%d",sizeof(i));
}
```

Answer:

sizeof(i)=1

Explanation:

Since the #define replaces the string int by the macro char

14.
```
main()
{
    int i=10;
    i=!i>14;
    Printf ("i=%d",i);
}
```

Answer:

i=0

Explanation:

In the expression !i>14 , NOT (!) operator has more precedence than ' >' symbol. ! is a unary logical operator. !i (!10) is 0 (not of true is false). 0>14 is false (zero).

15.
```
#include<stdio.h>
main()
{
    char s[]={'a','b','c','\n','c','\0'};
    char *p,*str,*str1;
    p=&s[3];
    str=p;
    str1=s;
    printf("%d",++*p + ++*str1-32);
}
```

Answer:

77

Explanation:

p is pointing to character '\n'. str1 is pointing to character 'a' ++*p. "p is pointing to '\n' and that is incremented by one." the ASCII value of '\n' is 10, which is then incremented to 11. The value of ++*p is 11. ++*str1, str1 is pointing to 'a' that is incremented by 1 and it becomes 'b'. ASCII value of 'b' is 98.

Now performing (11 + 98 - 32), we get 77("M");

So, we get the output 77 :: "M" (Ascii is 77).

16.
```
#include<stdio.h>
main()
{
    int a[2][2][2] = { {10,2,3,4}, {5,6,7,8} };
    int *p,*q;
    p=&a[2][2][2];
    *q=***a;
    printf("%d----%d",*p,*q);
}
```

Answer:

SomeGarbageValue---1

Explanation:

p=&a[2][2][2] you declared only two 2D arrays, but you are trying to access the third 2D(which you have not declared). It will print garbage values. *q=***a starting address of a is assigned integer pointer. Now q is pointing to starting address of a. If you print *q, it will print the first element of 3D array.

17.
```
#include<stdio.h>
main()
{
    struct xx
    {
        int x=3;
        char name[]="hello";
    };
    struct xx *s;
    printf("%d",s->x);
    printf("%s",s->name);
}
```

Answer:

Compiler Error

Explanation:

You should not initialise variables in declaration

18.
```
#include<stdio.h>
main()
{
    struct xx
    {
    int x;
    struct yy
    {
        char s;
        struct xx *p;
    };
    struct yy *q;
    };
}
```

Answer:

Compiler Error

Explanation:

The structure yy is nested within structure xx. Hence, the elements are of yy are to be accessed through the instance of structure xx, which needs an instance of yy to be known. If the instance is created after defining the structure the compiler will not know about the instance relative to xx. Hence, for nested structure yy you have to declare member.

19.
```
main()
{
    printf("\nab");
    printf("\bsi");
    printf("\rha");
}
```

Answer:

hai

Explanation:

\n - newline

\b - backspace

\r - linefeed

```
20. main()
{
int i=5;
printf("%d%d%d%d%d%d",i++,i--,++i,--i,i);
}
```

Answer:

45545

Explanation:

The arguments in a function call are pushed into the stack from left to right. The evaluation is by popping out from the stack and the evaluation is from right to left, hence the result.

```
21. #define square(x) x*x
    main()
    {
        int i;
        i = 64/square(4);
        printf("%d",i);
    }
```

Answer:

64

Explanation:

The macro call square(4) will substituted by 4*4 so the expression becomes i = 64/4*4 . Since / and * has equal priority the expression will be evaluated as (64/4)*4 i.e., 16*4 = 64

22.
```
main()
{
    char *p="hai friends",*p1;
    p1=p;
    while(*p!='\0') ++*p++;
    printf("%s   %s",p,p1);
}
```

Answer:

ibj!gsjfoet

Explanation:

++*p++ will be parse in the given order

*p that is value at the location currently pointed by p will be taken

++*p the retrieved value will be incremented

when ; is encountered the location will be incremented that is p++ will be executed

Hence, in the while loop initial value pointed by p is 'h', which is changed to 'i' by executing ++*p and pointer moves to point, 'a' which is similarly changed to 'b' and so on. Similarly, blank space is converted to '!'. Thus, we obtain value in p becomes "ibj!gsjfoet" and since p reaches '\0' and p1 points to p thus p1does not print anything.

23.
```
#include <stdio.h>
#define a 10
main()
{
    #define a 50
    printf("%d",a);
}
```

Answer:

50

Explanation:

The pre-processor directives can be redefined anywhere in the program. So, the most recently assigned value will be taken.

24.
```
#define clrscr() 100
main()
{
    clrscr();
    printf("%d\n",clrscr());
}
```

Answer:

100

Explanation:

Pre-processor executes as a separate pass before the execution of the compiler. So, textual replacement of clrscr().to 100 occurs.The input program to compiler looks like this :

```
main()
{
    100;
    printf("%d\n",100);
}
```

Note:

100; is an executable statement but with no action. So, it doesn't give any problem.

25.
```
main()
{
    printf("%p",main);
}
```

Answer:

Some address will be printed.

Explanation:

Function names are just addresses (just like array names are addresses).

main() is also a function. So, the address of function main will be printed. %p in printf specifies that the argument is an address. They are printed as hexadecimal numbers.

26
```
main()
{
clrscr();
}
clrscr();
```

Answer:

No output/error

Explanation:

The first clrscr() occurs inside a function. So, it becomes a function call. In the second clrscr(); is a function declaration (because it is not inside any function).

27
```
enum colours {BLACK,BLUE,GREEN}
main()
{
printf("%d..%d..%d",BLACK,BLUE,GREEN);
return(1);
}
```

Answer:

0..1..2

Explanation:

enum assigns numbers starting from 0, if not explicitly defined.

28
```
void main()
{
char far *farther,*farthest;
printf("%d..%d",sizeof(farther),sizeof(farthest));
}
```

Answer:

4..2

Explanation:

The second pointer is of char type and not a far pointer.

29
```
main()
{
int i=400,j=300;
printf("%d..%d");
}
```

Answer:

400..300

Explanation:

printf takes the values of the first two assignments of the program. Any number of printf's may be given. All of them take only the first two values. If more number of assignments given in the program, then printf will take garbage values.

30
```
main()
{
char *p;
p="Hello";
printf("%c\n",*&*p);
}
```

Answer:

H

Explanation:

* is a de-reference operator & is a reference operator. They can be applied any number of times provided it is meaningful. Here p points to the first character in the string "Hello". *p de-references it and so its value is H. Again & references it to an address and * de-references it to the value H.

31 main()

```
main()
{
    int i=1;
    while (i<=5)
    {
        printf("%d",i);
        if (i>2)
            goto here;
        i++;
    }
}
fun()
{
    here:
    printf("PP");
}
```

Answer:

Compiler error: Undefined label 'here' in function main.

Explanation:

Labels have functions scope. In other words, the scope of the labels is limited to functions. The label 'here' is available in function fun() Hence, it is not visible in function main.

32

```
main()
{
    static char names[5][20]={"pascal","ada","cobol","fortran","perl"};
    int i;
    char *t;
    t=names[3];
    names[3]=names[4];
    names[4]=t;
    for (i=0;i<=4;i++)
        printf("%s",names[i]);
}
```

Answer:

Compiler error: Lvalue required in function main.

Explanation:

Array names are pointer constants. So, they cannot be modified.

33

```
void main()
{
    int i=5;
    printf("%d",i++ + ++i);
}
```

Answer:

Output cannot be predicted exactly.

Explanation:

Side effects are involved in the evaluation of i

34

```
void main()
{
    int i=5;
    printf("%d",i+++++i);
}
```

Answer:

Compiler error

Explanation:

The expression i+++++i is parsed as i ++ ++ + i which is an illegal combination of operators.

35

```
#include<stdio.h>
main()
{
int i=1,j=2;
switch(i)
{
case 1:  printf("GOOD");
    break;
case j:  printf("BAD");
    break;
}
}
```

Answer:

Compiler error: Constant expression required in function main.

Explanation:

The case statement can have only constant expressions (this implies that we cannot use variable names directly so an error).

Note:

Enumerated types can be used in case statements.

36
```
main()
{
int i;
printf("%d",scanf("%d",&i));  * value 10 is given as input here*
}
```

Answer:

1

Explanation:

Scanf returns number of items successfully read and not 1/0. Here 10 is given as input which should have been scanned successfully. So, number of items read as 1.

37
```
#define f(g,g2) g##g2
main()
{
int var12=100;
printf("%d",f(var,12));
}
```

Answer:

100

38
```
main()
{
int i=0;
for(;i++;printf("%d",i)) ;
printf("%d",i);
}
```

Answer:

1

Explanation:

Before entering into the for loop the checking condition is "evaluated". Here it evaluates to 0 (false) and comes out of the loop, and i is incremented (note the semicolon after the for loop).

39
```
#include<stdio.h>
main()
{
    char s[]={'a','b','c','\n','c','\0'};
    char *p,*str,*str1;
    p=&s[3];
    str=p;
    str1=s;
    printf("%d",++*p + ++*str1-32);
}
```

Answer:

M

Explanation:

p is pointing to character '\n'.str1 is pointing to character 'a' ++*p meAnswer:"p is pointing to '\n' and that is incremented by one." The ASCII value of '\n' is 10. Then it is incremented to 11. The value of ++*p is 11. ++*str1 meAnswer:"str1 is pointing to 'a' that is incremented by 1 and it becomes 'b'. ASCII value of 'b' is 98. Both 11 and 98 is added and result is subtracted from 32.

i.e., (11+98-32)=77("M");

40
```
#include<stdio.h>
main()
{
    struct xx
    {
        int x=3;
        char name[]="hello";
    };
    struct xx *s=malloc(sizeof(struct xx));
    printf("%d",s->x);
    printf("%s",s->name);
}
```

Answer:

Compiler error

Explanation:

Initialisation should not be done for structure members inside the structure declaration.

41
```
#include<stdio.h>
main()
{
struct xx
{
    int x;
    struct yy
    {
      char s;
      struct xx *p;
      };
            struct yy *q;
  };
  }
```

Answer:

Compiler error

Explanation:

In the end of nested structure yy a member have to be declared.

42
```
main()
{
extern int i;
i=20;
printf("%d",sizeof(i));
}
```

Answer:

Linker error: Undefined symbol '_i'.

Explanation:

Extern declaration specifies that the variable i is defined somewhere else. The compiler passes the external variable to be resolved by the linker. So, compiler doesn't find an error. During linking the linker searches for the definition of i. Since it is not found, the linker flags an error.

43
```
main()
{
printf("%d", out);
}
int out=100;
```

Answer:

Compiler error: Undefined symbol out in function main.

Explanation:

The rule is that a variable is available for use from the point of declaration. Even though a is a global variable, it is not available for main. Hence, the error.

44
```
main()
{
extern out;
printf("%d", out);
}
int out=100;
```

Answer:

100

Explanation:

This is the correct way of writing the previous program.

45
```
main()
{
show();
}
void show()
{
printf("I'm the greatest");
}
```

Answer:

Compiler error: Type mismatch in redeclaration of show.

Explanation:

When the compiler sees the function show it doesn't know anything about it. So, the default return type (i.e., int) is assumed. But when compiler sees the actual definition of show mismatch occurs since it is declared as void. Hence, the error.

The solutions are as follows:

1. declare void show() in main().
2. define show() before main().
3. declare extern void show() before the use of show().

46
```
main( )
{
    int a[2][3][2] = {{{2,4},{7,8},{3,4}},{{2,2},{2,3},{3,4}}};
printf("%u %u %u %d \n",a,*a,**a,***a);
    printf("%u %u %u %d \n",a+1,*a+1,**a+1,***a+1);
}
```

Answer:

100, 100, 100, 2

114, 104, 102, 3

Explanation:

The given array is a 3-D one. It can also be viewed as a 1-D array.

2	4	7	8	3	4	2	2	2	3	3	4
100	102	104	106	108	110	112	114	116	118	120	122

thus, for the first printf statement a, *a, **a gives address of first element. Since the indirection ***a gives the value. Hence, the first line of the output. For the second printf a+1 increases in the third dimension thus points to value at 114, *a+1 increments in second dimension thus points to 104, **a +1 increments the first dimension thus points to 102 and ***a+1 first gets the value at first location and then increments it by 1. Hence, the output.

47
```
main( )
{
 int a[ ] = {10,20,30,40,50},j,*p;
for(j=0; j<5; j++)
{
    printf("%d" ,*a);
    a++;
```

```
        }
        p = a;
        for(j=0; j<5; j++)
          {
      printf("%d " ,*p);
     p++;
          }
     }
```

Answer:

Compiler error: lvalue required.

Explanation:

Error is in line with statement a++. The operand must be an lvalue and may be of any of scalar type for the any operator, array name only when subscripted is an lvalue. Simply array name is a non-modifiable lvalue.

48

```
main( )
{
 static int  a[ ]  = {0,1,2,3,4};
 int *p[ ] = {a,a+1,a+2,a+3,a+4};
 int **ptr =  p;
 ptr++;
 printf("\n %d  %d  %d", ptr-p, *ptr-a, **ptr);
 *ptr++;
 printf("\n %d  %d  %d", ptr-p, *ptr-a, **ptr);
 *++ptr;
printf("\n %d  %d  %d", ptr-p, *ptr-a, **ptr);
++*ptr;
printf("\n %d  %d  %d", ptr-p, *ptr-a, **ptr);
 }
```

Answer:

111

222

333

344

Explanation:

Let us consider the array and the two pointers with some address

a

0	1	2	3	4
100	102	104	106	108

P

100	102	104	106	108
1000	1002	1004	1006	1008

ptr

1000

2000

After execution of the instruction ptr++ value in ptr becomes 1002, if scaling factor for integer is 2 bytes. Now ptr - p is value in ptr - starting location of array p, (1002 - 1000) / (scaling factor) = 1, *ptr - a = value at address pointed by ptr - starting value of array a, 1002 has a value 102 so, the value is (102 - 100)/(scaling factor) = 1, **ptr is the value stored in the location pointed by the pointer of ptr = value pointed by 1002 = value pointed by 102 = 1. Hence, the output of the first printf is 1, 1, 1. After execution of *ptr++ increments value of the value in ptr by scaling factor, so it becomes1004. Hence, the output for the second printf are ptr - p = 2, *ptr - a = 2, **ptr = 2. After execution of *++ptr increments value of the value in ptr by scaling factor, so it becomes1004. Hence, the output for the third printf are ptr - p = 3, *ptr - a = 3, **ptr = 3. After execution of ++*ptr value in ptr remains the same, the value pointed by the value is incremented by the scaling factor. So, the value in array p at location 1006 changes from 106 10 108,. Hence, the output for the fourth printf are ptr - p = 1006 - 1000 = 3, *ptr - a = 108 - 100 = 4, **ptr = 4.

49

```
main( )
{
char *q;
int j;
for (j=0; j<3; j++) scanf("%s" ,(q+j));
for (j=0; j<3; j++) printf("%c" ,*(q+j));
for (j=0; j<3; j++) printf("%s" ,(q+j));
}
```

Explanation:

Here, we have only one pointer to type char and since we take input in the same pointer thus we keep writing over in the same location, each time shifting the pointer value by 1. Suppose the inputs are MOUSE, TRACK and VIRTUAL. Then for the first input suppose the pointer starts at location 100 then the input one is stored as:

When the second input is given the pointer is incremented as j value becomes 1, so the input is filled in memory starting from 101.

|M|O|U|S|E|\0|

|M|T|R|A|C|K| \0|

The third input starts filling from the location 102

|M|T|I| R|T|U| A|L|\0|

This is the final value stored.

The first printf prints the values at the position q, q+1 and q+2 = M T V

The second printf prints three strings starting from locations q, q+1, q+2

i.e., MTVIRTUAL, TVIRTUAL and VIRTUAL.

50

```
main( )
{
void *vp;
char ch = 'g', *cp = "goofy";
int j = 20;
vp = &ch;
printf("%c", *(char *)vp);
vp = &j;
printf("%d",*(int *)vp);
vp = cp;
printf("%s",(char *)vp + 3);
}
```

Answer:

g20fy

Explanation:

Since a void pointer is used it can be type casted to any other type pointer. vp = &ch stores address of char ch and the next statement prints the value stored in vp after type casting it to the proper data type pointer. The output is 'g'. Similarly, the output from second printf is '20'. The third printf statement type casts it to print the string from the 4th value hence the output is 'fy'.

51
```
main ( )
{
static char *s[ ]  = {"black", "white", "yellow", "violet"};
char **ptr[ ] = {s+3, s+2, s+1, s}, ***p;
p = ptr;
**++p;
printf("%s",*--*++p + 3);
}
```

Answer:

ck

Explanation:

In this problem we have an array of char pointers pointing to start of 4 strings. Then we have ptr which is a pointer to a pointer of type char and a variable p which is a pointer to a pointer of type char. p hold the initial value of ptr, i.e., p = s+3. The next statement increment value in p by 1 , thus now value of p = s+2. In the printf statement the expression is evaluated *++p causes gets value s+1 then the pre-decrement is executed and we get s+1 - 1 = s . The indirection operator now gets the value from the array of s and adds 3 to the starting address. The string is printed starting from this position. Thus, the output is 'ck'.

52
```
main()
{
int  i, n;
char *x = "girl";
n = strlen(x);
*x = x[n];
for(i=0; i<n; ++i)
  {
printf("%s\n",x);
x++;
  }
}
```

Answer:

(blank space)

irl

rl

l

Explanation:

Here a string (a pointer to char) is initialised with a value "girl". The strlen function returns the length of the string, thus n has a value 4. The next statement assigns value at the nth location ('\0') to the first location. Now the string becomes "\0irl" . Now the printf statement prints the string after each iteration it increments it starting position. Loop starts from 0 to 4. The first time x[0] = '\0' hence it prints nothing and pointer value is incremented. The second time it prints from x[1] i.e., "irl" and the third time it prints "rl" and the last time it prints "l" and the loop terminates.

53

```
int i,j;
 for(i=0;i<=10;i++)
 {
 j+=5;
 assert(i<5);
 }
```

Answer:

Runtime error: Abnormal program termination.

assert failed (i<5), <file name>,<line number>

Explanation:

Asserts are used during debugging to make sure that certain conditions are satisfied. If assertion fails, the program will terminate reporting the same. After debugging use,

#undef NDEBUG

and this will disable all the assertions from the source code. Assertion is a good debugging tool to make use of.

54

```
main()
{
int i=-1;
+i;
printf("i = %d, +i = %d \n",i,+i);
}
```

Answer:

i = -1, +i = -1

Explanation:

Unary + is the only dummy operator in C. Wherever it comes you can just ignore it because it has no effect in the expressions (hence the name dummy operator).

55 What are the files which are automatically opened when a C file is executed?

Answer:

stdin, stdout, stderr (standard input,standard output,standard error).

56 what will be the position of the file marker?

```
a: fseek(ptr,0,SEEK_SET);
b: fseek(ptr,0,SEEK_CUR);
```

Answer:

a: The SEEK_SET sets the file position marker to the starting of the file.

b: The SEEK_CUR sets the file position marker to the current position of the file.

57

```
main()
{
 char name[10],s[12];
 scanf(" \"%[^\"]\"",s);
}
```

How scanf will execute?

Answer:

First it checks for the leading white space and discards it. Then it matches with a quotation mark and then it reads all character up to another quotation mark.

58 What is the problem with the following code segment?

```
while ((fgets(receiving array,50,file_ptr)) != EOF)
        ;
```

Answer and Explanation:

fgets returns a pointer. So, the correct end of file check is checking for != NULL.

59 main()

```
{
main();
}
```

Answer:

Runtime error : Stack overflow.

Explanation:

Main function calls itself again and again. Each time the function is called its return address is stored in the call stack. Since there is no condition to terminate the function call, the call stack overflows at runtime. So, it terminates the program and results in an error.

60 main()

```
{
char *cptr,c;
void *vptr,v;
c=10;  v=0;
cptr=&c; vptr=&v;
printf("%c%v",c,v);
}
```

Answer:

Compiler error (at line number 4): size of v is unknown.

Explanation:

You can create a variable of type void * but not of type void, since void is an empty type. In the second line you are creating variable vptr of type void * and v of type void hence an error.

61 main()

```
{
char *str1="abcd";
char str2[]="abcd";
printf("%d %d %d",sizeof(str1),sizeof(str2),sizeof("abcd"));
}
```

Answer:

2 5 5

Explanation:

In first sizeof, str1 is a character pointer so it gives you the size of the pointer variable. In second sizeof the name str2 indicates the name of the array whose size is 5 (including the '\0' termination character). The third sizeof is similar to the second one.

62
```
main()
{
char not;
not=!2;
printf("%d",not);
}
```

Answer:

0

Explanation:

! is a logical operator. In C the value 0 is considered to be the boolean value FALSE, and any non-zero value is considered to be the boolean value TRUE. Here, 2 is a non-zero value so TRUE. !TRUE is FALSE (0) so it prints 0.

63
```
#define FALSE -1
#define TRUE   1
#define NULL   0
main() {
  if(NULL)
        puts("NULL");
  else if(FALSE)
        puts("TRUE");
  else
        puts("FALSE");
  }
```

Answer:

TRUE

Explanation:

The input program to the compiler after processing by the pre-processor is,

```
main(){
        if(0)
                puts("NULL");
else if(-1)
                puts("TRUE");
else
                puts("FALSE");
        }
```

Pre-processor doesn't replace the values given inside the double quotes. The check by if condition is boolean value false so it goes to else. In second if -1 is boolean value true hence "TRUE" is printed.

64

```
main()
{
int k=1;
printf("%d==1 is ""%s",k,k==1?"TRUE":"FALSE");
}
```

Answer:

1==1 is TRUE

Explanation:

When two strings are placed together (or separated by white-space) they are concatenated (this is called as "stringisation" operation). So, the string is as if it is given as "%d==1 is %s". The conditional operator(?:) evaluates to "TRUE".

65

```
main()
{
int y;
scanf("%d",&y); // input given is 2000
if( (y%4==0 && y%100 != 0) || y%100 == 0 )
     printf("%d is a leap year");
else
     printf("%d is not a leap year");
}
```

Answer:

2000 is a leap year

Explanation:

An ordinary program to check if leap year or not.

66
```
#define max 5
#define int arr1[max]
main()
{
 typedef char arr2[max];
 arr1 list={0,1,2,3,4};
 arr2 name="name";
 printf("%d %s",list[0],name);
}
```

Answer:

Compiler error (in the line arr1 list = {0,1,2,3,4})

Explanation:

arr2 is declared of type array of size 5 of characters. So, it can be used to declare the variable name of the type arr2. But it is not the case of arr1. Hence an error.

Rule of Thumb:

#defines are used for textual replacement, whereas typedefs are used for declaring new types.

67
```
int i=10;
main()
{
 extern int i;
  {
    int i=20;
      {
        const volatile unsigned i=30;
        printf("%d",i);
      }
    printf("%d",i);
  }
 printf("%d",i);
}
```

Answer:

30,20,10

Explanation:

'{' introduces new block and thus new scope. In the innermost block i is declared as, **const volatile unsigned** which is a valid declaration. i is assumed of type int. So, printf prints 30. In the next block, i has value 20 and so printf prints 20. In the outermost block, i is declared as extern, so no storage space is allocated for it. After compilation is over the linker resolves it to global variable i (since it is the only variable visible there). So, it prints i's value as 10.

68
```
main()
 {
    int *j;
    {
     int i=10;
     j=&i;
     }
     printf("%d",*j);
}
```

Answer:

10

Explanation:

The variable i is a block level variable and the visibility is inside that block only. But the lifetime of i is lifetime of the function so it lives up to the exit of main function. Since the i is still allocated space, *j prints the value stored in i since j points to i.

69
```
main()
 {
 int i=-1;
 -i;
 printf("i = %d, -i = %d \n",i,-i);
 }
```

Answer:

i = -1, -i = 1

Explanation:

-i is executed and this execution doesn't affect the value of i. In printf first you just print the value of i. After that the value of the expression -i = -(-1) is printed.

70 #include<stdio.h>

```
main()
{
const int i=4;
float j;
j = ++i;
printf("%d %f", i,++j);
}
```

Answer:

Compiler error

Explanation:

i is a constant. you cannot change the value of constant.

71 #include<stdio.h>

```
main()
{
 int a[2][2][2] = { {10,2,3,4}, {5,6,7,8} };
int *p,*q;
p=&a[2][2][2];
*q=***a;
printf("%d..%d",*p,*q);
}
```

Answer:

garbagevalue..1

Explanation:

p=&a[2][2][2] you declare only two 2D arrays. But you are trying to access the third 2D(which you have not declared) it will print garbage values. *q=***a starting address of a is assigned integer pointer. Now q is pointing to starting address of a. if you print *q meAnswer: it will print first element of 3D array.

72

```
#include<stdio.h>
main()
{
register i=5;
char j[]= "hello";
printf("%s  %d",j,i);
}
```

Answer:

hello 5

Explanation:

If you declare i as register compiler will treat it as ordinary integer and it will take integer value. i value may be stored either in register or in memory.

73

```
main()
{
  int i=5,j=6,z;
  printf("%d",i+++j);
}
```

Answer:

11

Explanation:

The expression i+++j is treated as (i++ + j)

75
```
struct aaa{
struct aaa *prev;
int i;
struct aaa *next;
};
main()
{
struct aaa abc,def,ghi,jkl;
int x=100;
abc.i=0;abc.prev=&jkl;
abc.next=&def;
def.i=1;def.prev=&abc;def.next=&ghi;
ghi.i=2;ghi.prev=&def;
ghi.next=&jkl;
jkl.i=3;jkl.prev=&ghi;jkl.next=&abc;
x=abc.next->next->prev->next->i;
printf("%d",x);
}
```

Answer:

2

Explanation:

All the above listed statements form a double circular linked list;

abc.next->next->prev->next->i

This one points to "ghi" node the value of at particular node is 2.

76
```
struct point
{
int x;
int y;
};
struct point origin,*pp;
main()
{
pp=&origin;
printf("origin is(%d%d)\n",(*pp).x,(*pp).y);
printf("origin is (%d%d)\n",pp->x,pp->y);
}
```

Answer:

origin is(0,0)
origin is(0,0)

Explanation:

pp is a pointer to structure. We can access the elements of the structure either with arrow mark or with indirection operator.

Note:

Since structure point is globally declared x & y are initialised as zeroes

77
```
main()
{
int i=_l_abc(10);
printf("%d\n",--i);
}
int _l_abc(int i)
{
return(i++);
}
```

Answer:

9

Explanation:

Return(i++) it will first return i and then increments, i.e., 10 will be returned.

78

```
main()
{
char *p;
int *q;
long *r;
p=q=r=0;
p++;
q++;
r++;
printf("%p...%p...%p",p,q,r);
}
```

Answer:

0001...0002...0004

Explanation:

++ operator when applied to pointers increments address according to their corresponding data-types.

79

```
main()
{
char c=' ',x,convert(z);
getc(c);
if((c>='a') && (c<='z'))
 x=convert(c);
printf("%c",x);
}
convert(z)
{
return z-32;
}
```

Answer:

Compiler error

Explanation:

Declaration of convert and format of getc() are wrong.

80
```
main(int argc, char **argv)
{
 printf("enter the character");
 getchar();
 sum(argv[1],argv[2]);
}
sum(num1,num2)
int num1,num2;
{
return num1+num2;
}
```

Answer:

Compiler error

Explanation:

argv[1] & argv[2] are strings. They are passed to the function sum without converting it to integer values.

81
```
# include <stdio.h>
 int one_d[]={1,2,3};
main()
{
int *ptr;
ptr=one_d;
ptr+=3;
printf("%d",*ptr);
}
```

Answer:

Garbagevalue

Explanation:

ptr pointer is pointing to out of the array range of one_d.

82

```
# include<stdio.h>
aaa() {
 printf("hi");
 }
bbb(){
printf("hello");
 }
ccc(){
 printf("bye");
 }
main()
{
 int (*ptr[3])();
 ptr[0]=aaa;
 ptr[1]=bbb;
 ptr[2]=ccc;
 ptr[2]();
 }
```

Answer:

bye

Explanation:

ptr is an array of pointers to functions of return type int. ptr[0] is assigned to address of the function aaa. Similarly, ptr[1] and ptr[2] for bbb and ccc respectively. ptr[2]() is in effect of writing ccc(), since ptr[2] points to ccc.

84

```
#include<stdio.h>
main()
{
FILE *ptr;
char i;
ptr=fopen("zzz.c","r");
 while((i=fgetch(ptr))!=EOF)
printf("%c",i);
}
```

Answer:

Contents of zzz.c followed by an infinite loop

Explanation:

The condition is checked against EOF. It should be checked against NULL.

85
```
main()
{
int i =0;j=0;
if(i && j++)
        printf("%d..%d",i++,j);
printf("%d..%d,i,j);
}
```

Answer:

0..0

Explanation:

The value of i is 0. Since this information is enough to determine the truth value of the boolean expression. So, the statement following the if statement is not executed. The values of i and j remain unchanged and get printed.

86
```
main()
{
int i;
i = abc();
printf("%d",i);
}
abc()
{
_AX = 1000;
}
```

Answer:

1000

Explanation:

Normally the return value from the function is through the information from the accumulator. Here _AH is the pseudo global variable denoting the accumulator. Hence, the value of the accumulator is set 1000 so the function returns value 1000.

87
```
int i;
main(){
int t;
for ( t=4;scanf("%d",&i)-t;printf("%d\n",i))
                printf("%d--",t--);
        }
// If the inputs are 0,1,2,3 find the o/p
```

Answer:

4--0

3--1

2--2

Explanation:

Let us assume some x= scanf("%d",&i)-t the values during execution will be,

t	i	x
4	0	-4
3	1	-2
2	2	0

88
```
main(){
int a= 0;int b = 20;char x =1;char y =10;
if(a,b,x,y)
printf("hello");
}
```

Answer:

hello

Explanation:

The comma operator has associativity from left to right. Only the rightmost value is returned and the other values are evaluated and ignored. Thus, y = 10 the value of last variable y is returned to check in if. Since it is a non-zero value it becomes true so, "hello" will be printed.

89

```
main(){
unsigned int i;
for(i=1;i>-2;i--)
        printf("c aptitude");
}
```

Explanation:

i is an unsigned integer. It is compared with a signed value. Since the both types do not match, signed is promoted to unsigned value. The unsigned equivalent of -2 is a huge value so condition becomes false and control comes out of the loop.

90 In the following pgm add a stmt in the function fun such that the address of 'a' gets stored in 'j'.

```
main(){
int * j;
void fun(int **);
fun(&j);
}
void fun(int **k) {
int a =0;
/* add a stmt here*/
}
```

Answer:

```
*k = &a
```

Explanation:

The argument of the function is a pointer to a pointer.

91 What are the following notations of defining functions known as?

i.
```
int abc(int a,float b)
{
/* some code */
}
```

ii.
```
int abc(a,b)
int a; float b;
{
/* some code*/
}
```

Answer:

i. ANSI C notation

ii. Kernighan & Ritchi notation

92
```
main()
{
char *p;
p="%d\n";
p++;
p++;
printf(p-2,300);
}
```

Answer:

300

Explanation:

The pointer points to % since it is incremented twice and again decremented by 2, it points to '%d\n' and 300 is printed.

93
```
main()
{
char a[100];
a[0]='a';a[1]]='b';a[2]='c';a[4]='d';
abc(a);
}
abc(char a[]){
a++;
   printf("%c",*a);
a++;
printf("%c",*a);
}
```

Explanation:

The base address is modified only in function and as a result a points to 'b' then after incrementing to 'c' so bc will be printed.

94
```
func(a,b)
int a,b;
{
        return( a= (a==b) );
}
main()
{
 int process(),func();
 printf("The value of process is %d !\n ",process(func,3,6));
}
process(pf,val1,val2)
int (*pf) ();
int val1,val2;
{
return((*pf) (val1,val2));
}
```

Answer:

The value if process is 0 !

Explanation:

The function 'process' has 3 parameters - 1, a pointer to another function 2 and 3, integers. When this function is invoked from main, the following substitutions for formal parameters take place: function for pf, 3 for val1 and 6 for val2. This function returns the result of the operation performed by the function 'func'. The function func has two integer parameters. The formal parameters are substituted as 3 for a and 6 for b. Since 3 is not equal to 6, a==b returns 0. Therefore, the function returns 0 which, in turn, is returned by the function 'process'.

95
```
void main()
{
static int i=5;
if(--i){
        main();
        printf("%d ",i);
}
}
```

Answer:

0 0 0 0

Explanation:

The variable "i" is declared as static, hence memory for i will be allocated for only once, as it encounters the statement. The function main() will be called recursively unless i becomes equal to 0, and since main() is recursively called, so the value of static i, i.e., 0 will be printed every time the control is returned.

96
```
void main()
{
 int k=ret(sizeof(float));
 printf("\n here value is %d",++k);
}
int ret(int ret)
{
ret += 2.5;
return(ret);
}
```

Answer:

Here value is 7

Explanation:

The int ret(int ret), i.e., the function name and the argument name can be the same. Firstly, the function ret() is called in which the sizeof(float) i.e., 4 is passed, after the first expression the value in ret will be 6, as ret is integer. Hence, the value stored in ret will have implicit type conversion from float to int. The ret is returned in main() it is printed after and pre-increment.

97
```
void main()
{
 char a[]="12345\0";
 int i=strlen(a);
 printf("here in 3 %d\n",++i);
}
```

Answer:

here in 3 6

Explanation:

The char array 'a' will hold the initialised string whose length will be counted from 0 till the null character. Hence, the 'i' will hold the value equal to 5, after the pre-increment in the printf statement, the 6 will be printed.

98
```
void main()
{
unsigned giveit=-1;
int gotit;
printf("%u ",++giveit);
printf("%u \n",gotit=--giveit);
}
```

Answer:

0 65535

99

```
void main()
{
int i;
 char a[]="\0";
 if(printf("%s\n",a))
            printf("Ok here \n");
else
            printf("Forget it\n");
}
```

Answer:

Ok here

Explanation:

Printf will return how many characters does it print. Hence, printing a null character returns 1 which makes the if statement true, thus "Ok here" is printed.

100

```
void main()
{
 void *v;
int integer=2;
int *i=&integer;
v=i;
printf("%d",(int*)*v);
}
```

Answer:

Compiler error. We cannot apply indirection on type void*.

Explanation:

Void pointer is a generic pointer type. No pointer arithmetic can be done on it. Void pointers are normally used for:

1. Passing generic pointers to functions and returning such pointers.
2. As an intermediate pointer type.
3. When the exact pointer type will be known at a later point of time.

101 void main()

```
{
int i=i++,j=j++,k=k++;
printf("%d%d%d",i,j,k);
}
```

Answer:

Garbage values.

Explanation:

An identifier is available to use in program code from the point of its declaration. So, expressions such as i = i++ are valid statements. The i, j and k are automatic variables and so they contain some garbage value. Garbage in is garbage out (GIGO).

102 void main()

```
{
  static int i=i++, j=j++, k=k++;
printf("i = %d j = %d k = %d", i, j, k);
}
```

Answer:

i = 1 j = 1 k = 1

Explanation:

Since static variables are initialised to zero by default.

103 void main()

```
{
  while(1){
        if(printf("%d",printf("%d")))
              break;
        else
              continue;
  }
}
```

Answer:

Garbage values

Explanation:

The inner printf executes first to print some garbage value. The printf returns no. of characters printed and this value also cannot be predicted. Still the outer printf prints something and so returns a non-zero value. So, it encounters the break statement and comes out of the while statement.

104

```
void main()
{
 unsigned int i=10;
 while(i-->=0)
        printf("%u ",i);
}
```

Answer:

10 9 8 7 6 5 4 3 2 1 0 65535 65534.....

Explanation:

Since i is an unsigned integer it can never become negative. So, the expression i-- >=0 will always be true, leading to an infinite loop.

105

```
#include<conio.h>
main()
{
 int x,y=2,z,a;
 if(x=y%2) z=2;
 a=2;
 printf("%d %d ",z,x);
}
```

Answer:

Garbage value 0

Explanation:

The value of y%2 is 0. This value is assigned to x. The condition reduces to if (x) or in other words if (0) and so z goes uninitialised.

Thumb Rule:

Check all control paths to write bug-free code.

106

```
main()
{
int a[10];
printf("%d",*a+1-*a+3);
}
```

Answer:

4

Explanation:

*a and -*a cancels out. The result is as simple as 1 + 3 = 4 !

107

```
#define prod(a,b) a*b
main()
{
int x=3,y=4;
printf("%d",prod(x+2,y-1));
}
```

Answer:

10

Explanation:

The macro expands and evaluates to as:

x+2*y-1 => x+(2*y)-1 => 10

108

```
main()
{
unsigned int i=65000;
while(i++!=0);
printf("%d",i);
}
```

Answer:

1

Explanation:

Note the semicolon after the while statement. When the value of i becomes 0 it comes out of while loop. Due to post-increment on i the value of i while printing is 1.

```
109   main()
      {
      int i=0;
      while(+(+i--)!=0)
            i-=i++;
      printf("%d",i);
      }
```

Answer:

-1

Explanation:

Unary + is the only dummy operator in C. So, it has no effect on the expression and now the while loop is, while(i--!=0) which is false and so breaks out of while loop. The value -1 is printed due to the post-decrement operator.

```
110   main()
      {
      float f=5,g=10;
      enum{i=10,j=20,k=50};
      printf("%d\n",++k);
      printf("%f\n",f<<2);
      printf("%lf\n",f%g);
      printf("%lf\n",fmod(f,g));
      }
```

Answer:

Line no. 5: Error: Lvalue required

Line no. 6: Cannot apply leftshift to float

Line no. 7: Cannot apply mod to float

Explanation:

Enumeration constants cannot be modified, so you cannot apply ++. Bit-wise operators and % operators cannot be applied on float values. fmod() is to find the modulus values for floats as % operator is for ints.

111

```
main()
{
int i=10;
  void pascal f(int,int,int);
f(i++,i++,i++);
        printf(" %d",i);
}
void pascal f(integer :i,integer:j,integer :k)
{
write(i,j,k);
}
```

Answer:

Compiler error: unknown type integer

Compiler error: undeclared function write

Explanation:

Pascal keyword does not mean that Pascal code can be used. It means that the function follows Pascal argument passing mechanism in calling the functions.

112

```
void pascal f(int i,int j,int k)
{
printf("%d %d %d",i, j, k);
}
void cdecl f(int i,int j,int k)
{
printf("%d %d %d",i, j, k);
}
main()
{
  int i=10;
f(i++,i++,i++);
printf(" %d\n",i);
i=10;
f(i++,i++,i++);
printf(" %d",i);
}
```

Answer:

10 11 12 13

12 11 10 13

Explanation:

Pascal argument passing mechanism forces the arguments to be called from left to right. cdecl is the normal C argument passing mechanism where the arguments are passed from right to left.

113 What is the output of the program given below

```
main()
  {
      signed char i=0;
      for(;i>=0;i++) ;
      printf("%d\n",i);
  }
```

Answer:

-128

Explanation:

Notice the semicolon at the end of the for loop. The initial value of the i is set to 0. The inner loop executes to increment the value from 0 to 127 (the positive range of char) and then it rotates to the negative value of -128. The condition in the for loop fails and so comes out of the for loop. It prints the current value of i that is -128.

114

```
main()
{
  unsigned char i=0;
  for(;i>=0;i++) ;
  printf("%d\n",i);
}
```

Answer:

infinite loop

Explanation:

The difference between the previous question and this one is that the char is declared to be unsigned. So, the i++ can never yield negative value and i>=0 never becomes false so that it can come out of the for loop.

115
```
main()
{
char i=0;
for(;i>=0;i++) ;
printf("%d\n",i);
}
```

Answer:

Behaviour is implementation-dependent.

Explanation:

The detail if the char is signed/unsigned by default is implementation-dependent. If the implementation treats the char to be signed by default the program will print -128 and terminate. On the other hand if it considers char to be unsigned by default, it goes to infinite loop.

Rule:

You can write programs that have implementation-dependent behaviour. But do not write programs that depend on such behaviour.

116 Is the following statement a declaration/definition. Find what does it mean?

```
int (*x)[10];
```

Answer:

Definition.

x is a pointer to array of (size 10) integers.

Apply clock-wise rule to find the meaning of this definition.

117 What is the output for the program given below

```
typedef enum errorType{warning, error, exception,}error;
main()
{
error g1;
g1=1;
printf("%d",g1);
}
```

Answer:

Compiler error: Multiple declaration for error

Explanation:

The name error is used in the two meanings. One means that it is a enumerator constant with value 1. The another use is that it is a type name (due to typedef) for enum errorType. Given a situation the compiler cannot distinguish the meaning of error to know in what sense the error is used:

```
error g1;
g1=error;
        // which error it refers in each case?
```

When the compiler can distinguish between usages then it will not issue error (in pure technical terms, names can only be overloaded in different namespaces).

Note: The extra comma in the declaration,

enum errorType{warning, error, exception,}

is not an error. An extra comma is valid and is provided just for programmer's convenience.

118

```
typedef struct error{int warning, error, exception;}error;
main()
{
  error g1;
  g1.error =1;
  printf("%d",g1.error);
}
```

Answer:

1

Explanation:

The three usages of name errors can be distinguishable by the compiler at any instance, so valid (they are in different namespaces).

Typedef struct error{int warning, error, exception;}error;

This error can be used only by preceding the error by struct keyword as in:

struct error someError;

typedef struct error{int warning, error, exception;}error;

This can be used only after . (dot) or -> (arrow) operator preceded by the variable name as in:

```
g1.error =1;
printf("%d",g1.error);
typedef struct error{int warning, error, exception;}error;
```

This can be used to define variables without using the preceding struct keyword as in:

error g1;

Since the compiler can perfectly distinguish between these three usages, it is perfectly legal and valid.

Note:

This code is given here to just explain the concept behind. In real programming do not use such overloading of names. It reduces the readability of the code. Possible does not mean that we should use it!

119
```
#ifdef something
int some=0;
#endif

main()
{
int thing = 0;
printf("%d %d\n", some ,thing);
}
```

Answer:

Compiler error : Undefined symbol some

Explanation:

This is a very simple example for conditional compilation. The name something is not already known to the compiler making the declaration

int some = 0;

effectively removed from the source code.

120
```
#if something == 0
int some=0;
#endif

main()
{
int thing = 0;
printf("%d %d\n", some ,thing);
}
```

Answer:

0 0

Explanation:

This code is to show that pre-processor expressions are not the same as the ordinary expressions. If a name is not known the pre-processor treats it to be equal to zero.

121 What is the output for the following program

```
main()
            {
 int arr2D[3][3];
   printf("%d\n", ((arr2D==* arr2D)&&(* arr2D == arr2D[0])) );
   }
```

Answer:

1

Explanation:

This is due to the close relation between the arrays and pointers. N dimensional arrays are made up of (N-1) dimensional arrays.

arr2D is made up of a 3 single arrays that contains 3 integers each .

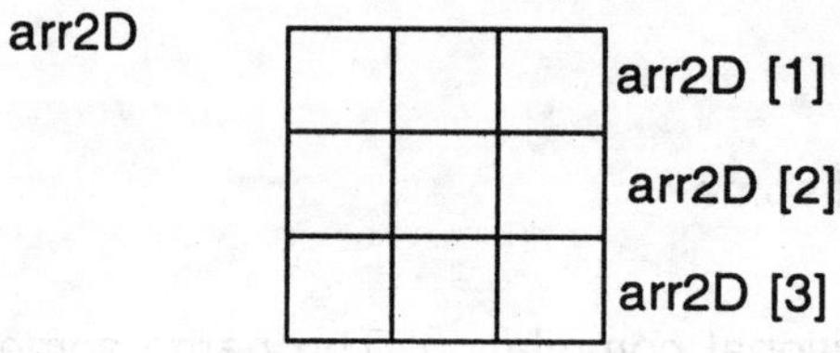

The name arr2D refers to the beginning of all the 3 arrays. *arr2D refers to the start of the first 1D array (of 3 integers) that is the same address as arr2D. So, the expression (arr2D == *arr2D) is true (1).

Similarly, *arr2D is nothing but *(arr2D + 0), adding a zero does not change the value/ meaning. Again arr2D[0] is the another way of telling *(arr2D + 0). So, the expression (*(arr2D + 0) == arr2D[0]) is true (1).

Since both parts of the expression evaluates to true the result is true(1) and the same is printed.

122
```
void main()
{
if(~0 == (unsigned int)-1)
printf("You can answer this if you know how values are represented in memory");
}
```

Answer:

You can answer this if you know how values are represented in memory

Explanation:

~ (tilde operator or bit-wise negation operator) operates on 0 to produce all ones to fill the space for an integer. -1 is represented in unsigned value as all 1's and so both are equal.

123
```
int swap(int *a,int *b)
{
 *a=*a+*b;*b=*a-*b;*a=*a-*b;
}
main()
{
        int x=10,y=20;
        swap(&x,&y);
        printf("x= %d y = %d\n",x,y);
}
```

Answer:

x = 20 y = 10

Explanation:

This is one way of swapping two values. Simple checking will help understand this.

124
```
main()
{
char *p = "ayqm";
printf("%c",++*(p++));
}
```

Answer:

b

125
```
main()
{
int i=5;
 printf("%d",++i++);
}
```
Answer:

Compiler error: Lvalue required in function main

Explanation:

++i yields an rvalue. For postfix ++ to operate an lvalue is required.

126
```
main()
{
char *p = "ayqm";
char c;
c = ++*p++;
printf("%c",c);
}
```
Answer:

b

Explanation:

There is no difference between the expression ++*(p++) and ++*p++. Parenthesis just works as a visual clue for the reader to see which expression is first evaluated.

127
```
int aaa() {printf("Hi");}
int bbb(){printf("hello");}
iny ccc(){printf("bye");}

main()
{
int ( * ptr[3]) ();
ptr[0] = aaa;
ptr[1] = bbb;
ptr[2] =ccc;
ptr[2]();
}
```
Answer:

bye

Explanation:

int (* ptr[3])() says that ptr is an array of pointers to functions that takes no arguments and returns the type int. By the assignment ptr[0] = aaa; it means that the first function pointer in the array is initialised with the address of the function aaa. Similarly, the other two array elements also get initialised with the addresses of the functions bbb and ccc. Since ptr[2] contains the address of the function ccc, the call to the function ptr[2]() is same as calling ccc(). So, it results in printing "bye".

128

```
main()
{
int i=5;
printf("%d",i=++i ==6);
}
```

Answer:

1

Explanation:

The expression can be treated as i = (++i==6), because == is of higher precedence than = operator. In the inner expression, ++i is equal to 6 yielding true(1). Hence the result.

129

```
main()
{
        char p[ ]="%d\n";
p[1] = 'c';
printf(p,65);
}
```

Answer:

A

Explanation:

Due to the assignment p[1] = 'c' the string becomes, "%c\n". Since this string becomes the format string for printf and ASCII value of 65 is 'A', the same gets printed.

130

```
void ( * abc( int, void ( *def) () ) ) ();
```

Answer:

abc is a ptr to a function which takes 2 parameters .(a). an integer variable.(b). a ptrto a funtion which returns void. the return type of the function is void.

Explanation:

Apply the clock-wise rule to find the result.

131
```
main()
{
while (strcmp("some","some\0"))
printf("Strings are not equal\n");
}
```

Answer:

No output

Explanation:

Ending the string constant with \0 explicitly makes no difference. So "some" and "some\0" are equivalent. So, strcmp returns 0 (false) hence breaking out of the while loop.

132
```
main()
{
char str1[] = {'s','o','m','e'};
char str2[] = {'s','o','m','e','\0'};
while (strcmp(str1,str2))
printf("Strings are not equal\n");
}
```

Answer:

"Strings are not equal"

"Strings are not equal"

....

Explanation:

If a string constant is initialised explicitly with characters, '\0' is not appended automatically to the string. Since str1 does not have null termination, it treats whatever the values that are in the following positions as part of the string until it randomly reaches a '\0'. So, str1 and str2 are not the same, hence the result.

133 main()

```
{
int i = 3;
for (;i++=0;) printf("%d",i);
}
```

Answer:

Compiler error: Lvalue required.

Explanation:

As we know that increment operators return rvalues and hence it cannot appear on the left hand side of an assignment operation.

134 void main()

```
{
int *mptr, *cptr;
mptr = (int*)malloc(sizeof(int));
printf("%d",*mptr);
int *cptr = (int*)calloc(sizeof(int),1);
printf("%d",*cptr);
}
```

Answer:

Garbage value 0

Explanation:

The memory space allocated by malloc is uninitialised, whereas calloc returns the allocated memory space initialised to zeros.

135 void main()

```
{
static int i;
while(i<=10)
(i>2)?i++:i--;
        printf("%d", i);
}
```

Answer:

32767

Explanation:

Since i is static it is initialised to 0. Inside the while loop the conditional operator evaluates to false, executing i--. This continues till the integer value rotates to positive value (32767). The while condition becomes false and hence, comes out of the while loop, printing the i value.

136 main()

```
{
        int i=10,j=20;
      j = i, j?(i,j)?i:j:j;
        printf("%d %d",i,j);
}
```

Answer:

10 10

Explanation:

The Ternary operator (? :) is equivalent for if-then-else statement. So, the question can be written as:

```
            if(i,j)
                {
if(i,j)
                j = i;
            else
                j = j;
            }
        else
            j = j;
```

137 1. const char *a;

2. char* const a;

3. char const *a;

-Differentiate the above declarations.

Answer:

1. 'const' applies to char * rather than 'a' (pointer to a constant char)

   *a='F' : illegal

   a="Hi" : legal

2. 'const' applies to 'a' rather than to the value of a (constant pointer to char)

   *a='F' : legal

   a="Hi" : illegal

3. Same as 1.

138

```
main()
{
        int i=5,j=10;
    i=i&=j&&10;
        printf("%d %d",i,j);
}
```

Answer:

1 10

Explanation:

The expression can be written as i=(i&=(j&&10)); The inner expression (j&&10) evaluates to 1 because j==10. i is 5. i = 5&1 is 1. Hence the result.

139 main()

```
{
        int i=4,j=7;
    j = j || i++ && printf("YOU CAN");
        printf("%d %d", i, j);
}
```

Answer:

4 1

Explanation:

The boolean expression needs to be evaluated only till the true value of the expression is not known. j is not equal to zero itself means that the expression's true value is 1. Because it is followed by || and true || (anything) => true where (anything) will not be evaluated. So, the remaining expression is not evaluated and so the value of i remains the same.

Similarly, when && operator is involved in an expression, when any of the operands become false, the whole expression's true value becomes false and hence the remaining expression will not be evaluated.

false && (anything) => false where (anything) will not be evaluated.

140 main()

```
{
        register int a=2;
    printf("Address of a = %d",&a);
        printf("Value of a   = %d",a);
}
```

Answer:

Compier error: '&' on register variable

Rule to Remember:

& (address of) operator cannot be applied on register variables.

141
```
main()
{
    float i=1.5;
    switch(i)
    {
        case 1: printf("1");
        case 2: printf("2");
        default : printf("0");
    }
}
```

Answer:

Compiler error: Switch expression not integral

Explanation:

Switch statements can be applied only to integral types.

142
```
main()
{
    extern i;
    printf("%d\n",i);
    {
        int i=20;
        printf("%d\n",i);
    }
}
```

Answer:

Linker error: Unresolved external symbol i

Explanation:

The identifier i is available in the inner block and so using extern has no use in resolving it.

143 main()

```
{
        int a=2,*f1,*f2;
        f1=f2=&a;
          *f2+=*f2+=a+=2.5;
        printf("\n%d %d %d",a,*f1,*f2);
}
```

Answer:

16 16 16

Explanation:

f1 and f2 both refer to the same memory location a. So, changes through f1 and f2 ultimately affects only the value of a.

144 main()

```
{
char *p="GOOD";
char a[ ]="GOOD";
printf("\n sizeof(p) = %d, sizeof(*p) = %d, strlen(p) = %d", sizeof(p),
sizeof(*p), strlen(p));
printf("\n sizeof(a) = %d, strlen(a) = %d", sizeof(a), strlen(a));
}
```

Answer:

sizeof(p) = 2, sizeof(*p) = 1, strlen(p) = 4

sizeof(a) = 5, strlen(a) = 4

Explanation:

sizeof(p) => sizeof(char*) => 2

sizeof(*p) => sizeof(char) => 1

Similarly, sizeof(a) => sizeof the character array => 5

When sizeof operator is applied to an array it returns the sizeof the array and it is not the same as the sizeof the pointer variable. Here the sizeof(a) where a is the character array and the sizeof the array is 5 because the space necessary for the terminating NULL character should also be taken into account.

145 #define DIM(array, type) sizeof(array)/sizeof(type)

```
main()
{
int arr[10];
printf("The dimension of the array is %d", DIM(arr, int));
}
```

Answer:

10

Explanation:

The size of integer array of 10 elements is 10 * sizeof(int). The macro expands to sizeof(arr)/ sizeof(int) => 10 * sizeof(int) / sizeof(int) => 10.

146 int DIM(int array[])

```
{
return sizeof(array)/sizeof(int );
}
main()
{
int arr[10];
printf("The dimension of the array is %d", DIM(arr));
}
```

Answer:

1

Explanation:

Arrays cannot be passed to functions as arguments and only the pointers can be passed. So, the argument is equivalent to int * array (this is one of the very few places where [] and * usage are equivalent). The return statement becomes, sizeof(int *)/ sizeof(int) that happens to be equal in this case.

147 main()

```
main()
{
        static int a[3][3]={1,2,3,4,5,6,7,8,9};
        int i,j;
        static *p[]={a,a+1,a+2};
          for(i=0;i<3;i++)
        {
                for(j=0;j<3;j++)
                printf("%d\t%d\t%d\t%d\n",*(*(p+i)+j),
                *(*(j+p)+i),*(*(i+p)+j),*(*(p+j)+i));
          }
}
```

Answer:

```
1   1   1   1
2   4   2   4
3   7   3   7
4   2   4   2
5   5   5   5
6   8   6   8
7   3   7   3
8   6   8   6
9   9   9   9
```

Explanation:

((p+i)+j) is equivalent to p[i][j].

147 main()

```
{
    void swap();
    int x=10,y=8;
    swap(&x,&y);
    printf("x=%d y=%d",x,y);
}
void swap(int *a, int *b)
{
    *a ^= *b, *b ^= *a, *a ^= *b;
}
```

Answer:

x=10 y=8

Explanation:

Using ^ like this is a way to swap two variables without using a temporary variable and that too in a single statement.

Inside main(), void swap(); means that swap is a function that may take any number of arguments (not no arguments) and returns nothing. So, this doesn't issue a compiler error by the call swap(&x,&y); that has two arguments.

This convention is historically due to pre-ANSI style (referred to as Kernighan and Ritchie style) style of function declaration. In that style, the swap function will be defined as follows:

```
void swap()
int *a, int *b
{
    *a ^= *b, *b ^= *a, *a ^= *b;
}
```

where the arguments follow the (). So, naturally the declaration for swap will look like, void swap() which means the swap can take any number of arguments.

149 main()

```
{
    int i = 257;
    int *iPtr = &i;
    printf("%d %d", *((char*)iPtr), *((char*)iPtr+1) );
}
```

Answer:

1 1

Explanation:

The integer value 257 is stored in the memory as, 00000001 00000001, so the individual bytes are taken by casting it to char * and get printed.

150 main()

```
{
    int i = 258;
    int *iPtr = &i;
    printf("%d %d", *((char*)iPtr), *((char*)iPtr+1) );
}
```

Answer:

2 1

Explanation:

The integer value 257 can be represented in binary as, 00000001 00000001. Remember that the INTEL machines are 'small-endian' machines. Small-endian means that the lower order bytes are stored in the higher memory addresses and the higher order bytes are stored in lower addresses. The integer value 258 is stored in memory as: 00000001 00000010.

151 main()

```
{
    int i=300;
    char *ptr = &i;
    *++ptr=2;
    printf("%d",i);
}
```

Answer:

556

Explanation:

The integer value 300 in binary notation is: 00000001 00101100. It is stored in memory (small-endian) as: 00101100 00000001. Result of the expression *++ptr = 2 makes the memory representation as: 00101100 00000010. So, the integer corresponding to it is 00000010 00101100 => 556.

152

```
#include <stdio.h>
main()
{
char * str = "hello";
char * ptr = str;
char least = 127;
while (*ptr++)
        least = (*ptr<least ) ?*ptr :least;
  printf("%d",least);
}
```

Answer:

0

Explanation:

After 'ptr' reaches the end of the string the value pointed by 'str' is '\0'. So, the value of 'str' is less than that of 'least'. So, the value of 'least' finally is 0.

153 Declare an array of N pointers to functions returning pointers to functions returning pointers to characters?

Answer:

```
(char*(*)( )) (*ptr[N])( );
```

154 main()

```
{
struct student
{
char name[30];
struct date dob;
}stud;
struct date
    {
    int day,month,year;
};
scanf("%s%d%d%d", stud.rollno, &student.dob.day, &student.dob.month,
&student.dob.year);
}
```

Answer:

Compiler error: Undefined structure date

Explanation:

Inside the struct definition of 'student' the member of type struct date is given. The compiler does not have the definition of date structure (forward reference is not allowed in C in this case) so it issues an error.

155 main()

```
{
struct date;
struct student
{
char name[30];
struct date dob;
}stud;
struct date
{
int day,month,year;
};
scanf("%s%d%d%d", stud.rollno, &student.dob.day, &student.dob.month,
&student.dob.year);
}
```

Answer:

Compiler error: Undefined structure date

Explanation:

Only declaration of struct date is available inside the structure definition of 'student' but to have a variable of type struct date the definition of the structure is required.

156 There were 10 records stored in "somefile.dat" but the following program printed 11 names. What went wrong?

```
void main()
{
struct student
{
char name[30], rollno[6];
}stud;
FILE *fp = fopen("somefile.dat","r");
while(!feof(fp))
{
fread(&stud, sizeof(stud), 1 , fp);
puts(stud.name);
}
}
```

Explanation:

fread reads 10 records and prints the names successfully. It will return EOF only when fread tries to read another record and fails reading EOF (and returning EOF). So, it prints the last record again. After this only the condition feof(fp) becomes false, hence comes out of the while loop.

157 Is there any difference between the two declarations,

1. int foo(int *arr[]) and
2. int foo(int *arr[2])

Answer:

No

Explanation:

Functions can only pass pointers and not arrays. The numbers that are allowed inside the [] is just for more readability. So, there is no difference between the two declarations.

158 What is the subtle error in the following code segment?

```
void fun(int n, int arr[])
{
int *p=0;
int i=0;
while(i++<n)
                p = &arr[i];
*p = 0;
}
```

Answer and Explanation:

If the body of the loop never executes p is assigned no address. So, p remains NULL where *p =0 may result in problem (may rise to runtime error "NULL pointer assignment" and terminate the program).

159 What is wrong with the following code?

```
int *foo()
{
int *s = malloc(sizeof(int)100);
 assert(s != NULL);
return s;
}
```

Answer and Explanation:

Assert macro should be used for debugging and finding out bugs. The check s != NULL is for error/exception handling and for that assert should not be used. A plain if and the corresponding remedy statement has to be given.

1560 What is the hidden bug with the following statement?

```
assert(val++ != 0);
```

Answer and Explanation:

Assert macro is used for debugging and removed in release version. In assert, the expression involves side-effects. So, the behaviour of the code becomes different in case of debug version and the release version thus leading to a subtle bug.

Rule to Remember:

Do not use expressions that have side-effects in assert statements.

161
```
void main()
{
int *i = 0x400;  // i points to the address 400
*i = 0;          // set the value of memory location pointed by i;
}
```

Answer:

Undefined behaviour

Explanation:

The second statement results in undefined behaviour because it points to some location whose value may not be available for modification. This type of pointer in which the non-availability of the implementation of the referenced location is known as 'incomplete type'.

162
```
#define assert(cond) if(!(cond)) \
(fprintf(stderr, "assertion failed: %s, file %s, line %d \n",#cond,\
__FILE__,__LINE__), abort())

void main()
{
int i = 10;
if(i==0)
assert(i < 100);
else
    printf("This statement becomes else for if in assert macro");
}
```

Answer:

No output

Explanation:

The else part in which the printf is there becomes the else for if in the assert macro. Hence, nothing is printed.

The solution is to use conditional operator instead of if statement,

```
#define assert(cond) ((cond)?(0): (fprintf (stderr, "assertion failed: \ %s, file %s, line %d \n",#cond, __FILE__,__LINE__), abort()))
```

Note:

However, this problem of "matching with nearest else" cannot be solved by the usual method of placing the if statement inside a block like this,

```
#define assert(cond) { \
if(!(cond)) \
(fprintf(stderr, "assertion failed: %s, file %s, line %d \n",#cond,\
__FILE__,__LINE__), abort()) \
}
```

163 Is the following code legal?

```
struct a
{
        int x;
        struct a b;
}
```

Answer:

No

Explanation:

Is it not legal for a structure to contain a member that is of the same type as in this case. Because this will cause the structure declaration to be recursive without end.

164 Is the following code legal?

```
struct a
{
int x;
   struct a *b;
}
```

Answer:

Yes.

Explanation:

*b is a pointer to type struct a and so is legal. The compiler knows, the size of the pointer to a structure even before the size of the structure is determined (as you know the pointer to any type is of same size). This type of structures is known as 'self-referencing' structure.

165 Is the following code legal?

```
typedef struct a
    {
int x;
aType *b;
 }aType
```

Answer:

No

Explanation:

The typename aType is not known at the point of declaring the structure (forward references are not made for typedefs).

166 Is the following code legal?

```
typedef struct a aType;
struct a
{
int x;
aType *b;
};
```

Answer:

Yes

Explanation:

The typename aType is known at the point of declaring the structure, because it is already typedefined.

167 Is the following code legal?

```
void main()
{
typedef struct a aType;
aType someVariable;
struct a
{
int x;
    aType *b;
  };
}
```

Answer:

No

Explanation:

When the declaration, typedef struct a aType; is encountered body of struct a is not known. This is known as 'incomplete types'.

168
```
void main()
{
printf("sizeof (void *) = %d \n", sizeof( void *));
  printf("sizeof (int *)    = %d \n", sizeof(int *));
  printf("sizeof (double *)  = %d \n", sizeof(double *));
  printf("sizeof(struct unknown *) = %d \n", sizeof(struct unknown *));
 }
```

Answer:

```
sizeof (void *) = 2
sizeof (int *)    = 2
sizeof (double *)  =  2
sizeof(struct unknown *) =  2
```

Explanation:

The pointer to any type is of same size.

169
```
char inputString[100] = {0};
```

To get string input from the keyboard which one of the following is better?

1) gets(inputString)
2) fgets(inputString, sizeof(inputString), fp)

Answer and Explanation:

The second one is better because gets(inputString) doesn't know the size of the string passed and so, if a very big input (here, more than 100 chars) the character will be written past the input string. When fgets is used with stdin performs the same operation as gets but is safe.

170 Which version do you prefer of the following two,

```
1) printf("%s",str);      // or the more curt one
2) printf(str);
```

Answer and Explanation:

Prefer the first one. If the str contains any format character like %d then it will result in a subtle bug.

171

```
void main()
{
int i=10, j=2;
int *ip= &i, *jp = &j;
int k = *ip/*jp;
printf("%d",k);
}
```

Answer:

Compiler error: "Unexpected end of file in comment started in line 5".

Explanation:

The programmer intended to divide two integers, but by the "maximum munch" rule, the compiler treats the operator sequence / and * as /* which happens to be the starting of comment. To force what is intended by the programmer,

```
int k = *ip/ *jp;
// give space explicity separating / and *
//or
int k = *ip/(*jp);
// put braces to force the intention  will solve the problem.
```

172 void main()

```
{
char ch;
for(ch=0;ch<=127;ch++)
printf("%c   %d \n", ch, ch);
}
```

Answer:

Implementaion-dependent

Explanation:

The char type may be signed or unsigned by default. If it is signed then ch++ is executed after ch reaches 127 and rotates back to -128. Thus, ch is always smaller than 127.

173 Is this code legal?

```
int *ptr;
ptr = (int *) 0x400;
```

Answer:

Yes

Explanation:

The pointer ptr will point at the integer in the memory location 0x400.

174 main()

```
{
char a[4]="HELLO";
printf("%s",a);
}
```

Answer:

Compiler error: Too many initialisers

Explanation:

The array a is of size 4 but the string constant requires 6 bytes to get stored.

175
```
main()
{
char a[4]="HELL";
printf("%s",a);
}
```
Answer:

HELL%@!~@!@???@~~!

Explanation:

The character array has the memory just enough to hold the string "HELL" and does not have enough space to store the terminating null character. So, it prints the HELL correctly and continues to print garbage values till it accidentally comes across a NULL character.

176
```
main()
{
        int a=10,*j;
        void *k;
          j=k=&a;
        j++;
         k++;
        printf("\n %u %u ",j,k);
}
```
Answer:

Compiler error: Cannot increment a void pointer

Explanation:

Void pointers are generic pointers and they can be used only when the type is not known and as an intermediate address storage type. No pointer arithmetic can be done on it and you cannot apply indirection operator (*) on void pointers.

END

SECTION

VI: PUZZLES IN C

Objectives

In the previous section you have encountered the mental-processing paradigm required for a professional C programmer. This section continues on the same theme. The difference is here, purposely, explanations and answers are not provided. Wherever required, depending upon the difficulty level of the problem, suggestive notes are provided to help the readers. The readers can test their understanding of C language by solving the puzzles in this section on their own. In case of any difficulty refer back to the similar problems from previous section to enhance your understanding.

Contents:

Puzzles in C

1. Predict the output of following code snippet.

```
#include < stdio.h >
int main()
{
  float x = 0.2;

  if(x == 0.2F)
     printf("x is equal to 0.2\n");
else
     printf("x is not equal to 0.2\n");

return(0);
}
```

2. Predict the output of following code snippet.

```
#include < stdio.h >
int main()
{
  float x, y;
  x = y = 0.2;
  if(x == 0.2)
     printf("x is equal to 0.2\n");
  else
     printf("x is not equal to 0.2\n");
  if(x == y)
     printf("x is equal to y\n");
else
     printf("x is not equal to y\n");
return(0);
}
```

3. Predict the behaviour of following code snippet.

```
#include < stdio.h >
void f();
int main(void)
{
  f();
  return(0);
 }
 void f()
{
  printf("In f().\n");
   main();
 }
```

4. Differentiate between the following (with respect to C language):

```
int main(void)
int main(int argc, char *argv[])
int main(int argc, char *argv[], char *envp[])
main()
void main()
int main()
```

Hint:

Please refer to C99 standard.

5. Predict the output of following code snippet.

```
void main()
{
      unsigned char ch;
      FILE *fp;
      fp=fopen("institute.txt", "r");
      while((ch = fgetc(fp))!= EOF) printf("%c",ch);
      fclose(fp);
}
```

Assumption:

institute.txt exists and contains text Dr. Sachin Kadam

6. Predict the behaviour of following code snippet.

```
#include <stdio.h>
void f1()
{
    printf("In f1().\n");
    f2();
}
void f2()
{
    printf("In f2().\n");
    f3();
}
void f3()
{
    printf("In f3().\n");
}
main()
{
    f1();
}
```

7. Are the following C declarations same or different?

```
const char *p;
char* const p;
```

8. The expected output of the following C program is to print the elements in the array. But when actually run, it does not do so. Find out what is going wrong.

```
#include <stdio.h>
#define TOTAL_ELEMENTS (sizeof(array)/sizeof(array[0]))
int array[] = {23,34,12,17,204,99,16};
int main()
{
    int d;
    printf("%d\n", TOTAL_ELEMENTS);
    for(d=-1;d <= (TOTAL_ELEMENTS-2);d++) printf("%d\n",array[d+1]);
    return(0);
}
```

Hint:

Please go through the previous puzzles for clues.

9. Predict the output of following code snippet.

```
#include <stdio.h>
int main()
{
    float a;
    a = 5/3;
    printf("%f", a);
    return 0;
}
```

10. Predict the output of the following C program.

```
#include <stdio.h >
#define calc(a, b) (a * b) / (a - b)
int main()
{
    int a = 20, b = 10;
    printf("%d\n", calc(a + 4, b -2));
    return(0);
}
```

11. Predict the output of the following C program.

```
#include <stdio.h>
#define ABC 20
#define XYZ 10
#define XXX ABC - XYZ
int main()
{
    int a;
    a = XXX * 10;
    printf("%d\n", a);
    return(0);
}
```

12. Can the following C source code be compiled by most of the available C compilers?

```
#include < stdio.h >
#include < conio.h >
int main()
{
    clrscr();
    printf("hello world");
    return(0);
}
```

13. Is it a valid C program? If yes, then what will be its output?

```
#define oO(o) for (o=2; o
#define Oo(o) ; o++)
#define OO(O,o) if (O==o)
#define oo(o,O) oO(o) O Oo(o)
int main() { int o,O; oo(o,<100)
oo(O,<=o) OO(o,O) printf("%d ",o);
else OO(o%O,0) break; putchar('\n'); return 0; }
```

14. Predict the output of following code snippet.

```
int main()
{
 int a = 1;
switch(a)
{
   int b = 20;
   case 1: printf("In case 1: b = %d",b);
         break;
   default:printf("In default: b = %d",b);
        break;
}
return 0;
}
```

15. Case study:

1. A C program is split across multiple files (file1.c, file2.c, file3.c)
2. A variable is defined in file1.c and used in file2.c and file3.c.
3. All the three files need to be compiled together to get the final program.

Propose a strategy to fulfil these requirements.

16. Predict the output of the following C code snippet.

```
main(){char*p="main(){char*p=%c%s%c;(void)printf(p,34,p,34,10);}%c";(void)pr
intf(p,34,p,34,10);}
```

Hint:

1. Obfuscated C program
2. The whole program is a single line (i.e., without any newline character)

17. **Predict the output of following C code snippet?**

```
int main()
{
    int x = 1 //* */2
    ;
    printf("%d", x);
    return(0);
}
```

Hint:

It is a C code snippet.

18. **Are the following two function prototypes same with respect to C?**

```
int f1(void);
int f2();
```

19. **What is the functionality of following function?**

```
int f(unsigned int x)
{
    int count=0;
   while(x)
   {
      count++;
      x = x&(x-1);
   }
    return count;
}
```

20. Can you explain the strange behaviour of following code snippet?

```
int main()
{
    int a, b, c, d;
    a = 5;
    b = 10;
    c = a, b;
    d = (a, b);
    printf("c=%d : d=%d\n", c, d);
    return 0;
}
```

Hint:

Comma Operator in C

21. How to validate that the user provides appropriate input (required number of inputs along with proper data types) to a scanf( ) function?

---

22. What would be the output of following code snippet?

```
int main()
{
    int i;
    i = 43;
    printf("%d\n",printf("%d",printf("%d",i)));
    return 0;
}
```

Note:

It is a valid C program.

23. Predict the output of following code snippet.

```
int main()
{
    float f = 0.1;
    if(f == 0.1)
        printf("f is equal to 0.1\n");
    else
        printf("f is not equal to 0.1\n");
    return 0;
}
```

24. What is the functionality of following function?

```
int f(unsigned int x )
{
static unsigned int mask[] = { 0x55555555,
  0x33333333,
  0x0F0F0F0F,
  0x00FF00FF,
  0x0000FFFF
} ;

int i ;
int shift ;
 for ( i=0, shift=1; i<5; i++, shift*=2)
     x=(x & mask[i])+((x >> shift) & mask[i]);
return x;
}
```

Hint:

AND operator (to perform bit masking)

Shift operator (to perform bit shifting)

25. Predict the output for the following code snippet.

```
int main()
{
    int a=10;
    switch(a)
    {
        case '1':
            printf("ONE\n");
            break;
        case '2':
            printf("TWO\n");
            break;
        defa1ut:
            printf("NONE\n");
    }
    return 0;
}
```

Note:

The above code snippet does not give any compile-time or run-time error. It compiles and executes without a hitch.

26. Predict the output for the following code snippet.

```
#define f(a,b) a##b
#define g(a) #a
#define h(a) g(a)
int main()
{
    printf("%s\n",h(f(1,2)));
    printf("%s\n",g(f(1,2)));
    return 0;
}
```

Hint:

1. Both the outputs may appear to be the same, but that is not what we are going to get.
2. Look for the pre-processor directives.

SECTION

VII: OBJECTIVE TESTS ON C LANGUAGE

Objectives

This section tests the understanding of C language from objective perspective. It contains 3 objective tests. Each test contains 50 questions. Each question has four options, out of which the reader is supposed select the correct option(s). The correct answers are provided at the end of the each test. The reader is encouraged to take these tests in competitive spirit. Each test should be ideally timed for 60 minutes. At the end of the test the reader should compare the answers with the provided ones. To bridge the semantic gap in understanding refer back to the section on FAQs for similar kinds of problems.

Contents:

Objective Test-1

1. main()

```
{
int i;
printf("%d",scanf("%d",&i)); // value 10 is given as input here
}
```

   (a) 0
   (b) 2
   (c) 1
   (d) -1

2. int i,j;

```
for(i=0;i<=10;i++)
    {
    j+=5;
    assert(i<5);
    }
```

   (a) Compile error
   (b) Linker error
   (c) Runtime error
   (d) 01234

3. main()

```
{
char *str1="abcd";
char str2[]="abcd";
printf("%d %d %d",sizeof(str1),sizeof(str2),sizeof("abcd"));
}
```

   (a) 2 3 4
   (b) 2 5 5
   (c) 1 3 5
   (d) 0 2 4

4. When a 'C' function call is made, the order in which parameters passed to the function are pushed into the stack is

   (a) left to right
   (b) right to left

(c) bigger variables are moved first than the smaller variables.

(d) smaller variables are moved first than the bigger ones.

(e) none of the above.

5. Memory allocation of variables declared in a program is

(a) allocated in RAM.

(b) allocated in ROM.

(c) allocated on stack.

(d) assigned to registers.

6. main()

```
{
register i=5;
char j[]= "hello";
printf("%s  %d",j,i);
}
```

(a) 5 hello

(b) hello5

(c) 5hello

(d) hello 5

7. #define COND(a) if(a>=65 && a<=90)

main()

```
{
char ch='R';
COND(ch)
        printf("Upper case");
else
        printf("LOwer case");
}
```

(a) Error

(b) Upper case

(c) Lower case

(d) None

8. Pre-proconia.. does not do which one of the following
   (a) macro
   (b) conditional complication
   (c) in type checking
   (d) including load file

9.
```
#include<stdio.h>
#include<conio.h>
void main()
    {
    int k=35,z;
    k=func1(k=func1(k=func1(k)));
    printf("k=%d",k);
    }
func1(int k)
int k;
    {
     k++;
     return(k);
     }
```
   (a) k=38
   (b) k=35
   (c) k=36
   (d) error

10.
```
#include<stdio.h>
#include<conio.h>
void main()
    {
    int i=10;
    clrscr();
    &i=7200;
    printf("%d  %u",i,&i);
    getch();
    }
```

(a) 10 Garbage value

(b) 10 7200

(c) Error

(d) None of these

11.
```
#include<stdio.h>
void main()
    {
    float i=10,*j;
    void *k;
    k=&i;
    j=k;
    printf("\n%f",*j);
    }
```

(a) 10.000000

(b) some address

(c) compilation error

(d) none

12.
```
main()
    {
    window(20,10,40,20);
    #include "conio.h"
    cprintf("this is my mca class");
    cprintf("this is not my mca class");
    }
```

(a) Error

(b) this is my mca class
this is not my mca class

(c) This is my mca class

(d) This is not my mca class

13.

```
#define ISLOWER(((a) (a>=97 &&a<=127)
#define TOUPPER(((a) (a-32)
main()
    {
    char ch='c';
    if(ISLOWER(ch))
    ch=TOUPPER(ch)
    printf("%c",ch);
    }
```

(a) C

(b) D

(c) B

(d) A

14. In tree construction which is the suitable efficient data structure?

(a) Array

(b) Linked list

(c) Stack

(d) Queue

(e) none

15.

```
main()
    {
    int x=10, y=15;
    x = x++;
    y = ++y;
    printf("%d %d\n",x,y);
    }
```

(a) 11,16

(b) 11,14

(c) 11,15

(d) 11,17

16.
```
main()
{
int x=5;
printf("%d,%d,%d\n",x,x<<2,x>>2);
}
```
(a) 5,21,1

(b) 5,20,1

(c) 6,21,2

(d) 6,21,2

17.
```
main()
{
int x=20,y=35;
x=y++ + x++;
y= ++y + ++x;
printf("%d%d\n",x,y);
}
```
(a) 5793

(b) 5794

(c) 5795

(d) 5792

18. Which header file in C++ does contain function prototypes for memory allocation?

(a) <iostream.h>

(b) <stdio.h>

(c) <stdlib.h>

(d) <limits.h>

19. int x = 5;

int y = 7;

What is the value of x and y after the expression y+=x++;

(a) 14,7

(b) 13, 7

(c) 12, 6

(d) 11,12

20. What is the precedence order from high to low, of the symbols ( ) ++ /

(a) ( ) , ++, /

(b) ++, (), /

(c) /, (),++

(d) /, ++, ()

21.
```
#include<stdio.h>
main()
  {
  int arr[]={10,20,30,45,67,56,74};
  int *i,*j;
  i=&arr[1];
  j=&arr[5];
  printf("%d%d",j-i,*j-*i);
  }
```

(a) 10,36

(b) 5,36

(c) 4,36

(d) 4,57

22.
```
#include<stdio.h>
#include<conio.h>
void main()
  {
  int i=10;
  clrscr();
  &i=7200;
  printf("%d  %u",i,&i);
  getch();
  }
```

(a) 10 Garbage value

(b) 10 7200

(c) Error

(d) None of these

23. Of the following tree structure, which is efficient considering space and time complexities?

(a) incomplete Binary Tree

(b) Complete Binary Tree

(c) full Binary Tree

(d) Half Binary Tree

24. Find the output of the following program

```
int *p,*q;
p=(int *)1000;
q=(int *)2000;
printf("%d",(q-p));
```

(a) 234

(b) 500

(c) 300

(d) 400

25. In binary search tree which traversal is used for getting ascending order values

(a) Inorder

(b) Postorder

(c) Preorder

d) Heap Sort

26.
```
#include<stdio.h>
#include<conio.h>
void main()
        {
         int k=35,z;
         k=func1(k=func1(k=func1(k)));
        printf("k=%d",k);
        }
func1(int k)
int k;
        {
         k++;
         return(k);
        }
```

(a) k=38

(b) k=35

(c) k=36

(d) Error

27.
```
#define DATATYPE charfar*
main()
    {
     DATATYPE s;
     s=0Xb8000000;
     *s='A';
    }
```
(a) just the display of screen

(b) A

(c) error

(d) none of these

28.
```
main()
    {
    char not;
    not=!2;
    printf("%d",not);
    }
```
(a) Error

(b) 0

(c) not

(d) -1

29.
```
main()
    {
    int k=1;
    printf("%d==1 is ""%s",k,k==1?"TRUE":"FALSE");
    }
```
(a) True

(b) False

30. Find the output for the following C program

```
i=20,k=0;
for(j=1;j
    {
    k+=j<10?4:3;
    }
printf("%d", k);
```

(a) 1

(b) 2

(c) 3

(d) 4

31. The sign # is called:

(a) Header

(b) String

(c) Character

(d) Compiler directive

32. void main()

```
    {
    int d=5;
    printf("%f",d);
    }
```

(a) 5

(b) 5.000000

(c) Undefined

(d) Error

33. void main()

```
    {
    float j;
    j=1000*1000;
    printf("%f",j);
    }
```

(a) 1000000

(b) Overflow

(c) Error

(d) None

34. Find the output of the following C program

```
main()
    {
    char *p1="Name";
    char *p2;
    p2=(char *)malloc(20);
    while(*p2++=*p1++);
    printf("%s\n",p2);
    }
```

(a) Error

(b) 20

(c) An Empty String

(d) None of the above

35. struct list{

```
    int x;
    struct list *next;
    }*head;
```

the struct head.x =100

Is the above assignment to pointer is correct or wrong?

(a) True

(b) False

36. What will be the output of the program?

```
main()
    {
     long *ptr;
    printf("%ld",sizeof(ptr));
    }
```

(a) Error

(b) 8

(c) 2

(d) None of the above

37. What will be the output of the program?

```
main()
{
    int a[5]={1,2,3,4,5};
    int *ptr;
    ptr=a;
    printf("%d",*ptr):
    ptr+=10;
    printf("%d",*ptr):
}
```

(a) 1,5

(b) 1,0

(c) 1,Garbage value

(d) 1,15

38. Which of the following data can a pointer hold?

(a) integer

b) character

(c) integer and character

(d) int, char, float

39. scanf() is

(a) User defined function

(b) Library function

(c) (a) and (b)

(d) None of the above

40. fseek(fp,-1,SEEK_CUR), will move the pointer to the:

(a) End of the file.

(b) Will remain at same position of the pointer.

(c) Start of the file

(d) Error

(e) None of the above

41.
```
main()
{
char *str1="abcd";
char str2[]="abcd";
printf("%d %d %d",sizeof(str1),sizeof(str2),sizeof("abcd"));
}
```

(a) 2 3 4

(b) 1 3 5

(c) 2 5 5

(d) 0 2 4

42. What will be the output of the program?

```
main()
{
int *ptr=NULL;
if(*ptr==0)
        printf("YES");
else
        printf("NO");
}
```

(a) NULL

(b) Can not say

(c) YES

(d) NO

43. What will be the output of the program?

```
main()
    {
    int *a,*b;
    *a=4;
    *b=2;
    printf("*a / *b =%d ",*a/*b);
    getch();
    }
```

(a) *a/*b=2

(b) *a/*b=Division of address of a and b

(c) *a/*b=0

(d) None of the above

44. Find the output for the following C program

```
main()
    {
    char *p1="Name";
    char *p2;
    p2=(char *)malloc(20);
    while(*p2++=*p1++);
    printf("%s\n",p2);
    }
```

(a) Error

(b) 20

(c) An Empty String

(d) None of the above

45. Which kind of function is included in this #include <sys/stat.h> and #include <sys/types.h> header files:-

(a) Directory manipulation

(b) File manipulation

(c) String manipulation

(d) Buffer manipulation

46. What is the output of the following?

```
int i;
i=1;
i=i+2*i++;
printf(%d,i);
```

(a) 2

(b) 3

(c) 4

(d) 5

47. The type of the controlling statement of a switch statement cannot be of the type

(a) int

(b) char

(c) short

(d) float

48. What is the value assigned to the variable X if b is 7?

```
X = b>8 ? b <<3 : b>4 ? b>>1:b;
```

(a) 7

(b) 28

(c) 3

(d) 14

49. Which is the output produced by the following program

```
main()
    {
    int n=2;
    printf("%d %d\n", ++n, n*n);
    }
```

(a) 3,6

(b) 3,4

(c) 2,4

(d) can not determine

50. What is the output of the following problem?

```
#define INC(X) X++
main()
    {
    int X=4;
    printf("%d",INC(X++));
    }
```

(a) 4

(b) 5

(c) 6

(d) Compilation error

Answer Table

1	C	11	a	21	b	31	d	41	c
2	C	12	b	22	c	32	c	42	c
3	B	13	a	23	b	33	d	43	d
4	b	14	b	24	b	34	c	44	c
5	c	15	a	25	a	35	b	45	b
6	d	16	b	26	a	36	c	46	c
7	b	17	b	27	b	37	c	47	d
8	c	18	c	28	b	38	a	48	c
9	a	19	c	29	a	39	b	49	b
10	c	20	a	30	d	40	e	50	d

END

Objective Test-2

1. What is the size of the following union?

Assume that the size of int = 2, size of float = 4, and size of char =1.

```
Union Tag
    {
    int a;
    float b;
    char c;
    };
```

(a) 2

(b) 4

(c) 1

(d) 7

2.

```
int x=-0;
while (1)
    {
    x++;
    }
```

(a) Runs only once.

(b) Runs infinite number of times.

(c) Does not run at all.

(d) Gives compile time error.

3.

```
Main
    {
    while (x <= 50 = = 0)
    for(    ;       ;       )
            if(++x%50 = = 0)
                    break;
            printf(" x = %d",x);
    }
```

(a) Will print x = 50.

(b) Will give compilation error.

(c) Will give runtime error.

(d) Will print x = 100.

4. The break statement causes an exit.

(a) Only from the innermost loop

(b) Only from the innermost switch

(c) From the innermost loop or switch

(d) None of the above

5.
```
main()
{
int a=5,b=10;
int *ptr1=&a, *ptr2=&b;
prinf("%d",(*ptr1)+(*ptr2));
}
```

(a) 15

(b) garbage value

(c) error

(d) none of the above

6.
```
void main()
{
int a=1;
printf("%d%d",a,++a,a++);
}
```

(a) 123

(b) 122

(c) 133

(d) 331

7. Void Pointer is -----------.

(a) generic pointer

(b) int pointer

(c) char pointer

(d) Null pointer

8. Check valid or invalid!

```
int a;
int *p = 2 a;
scanf( " % d ", p ) ;
```

(a) Valid

(b) Invalid

9. Given

```
int a = 25;
int *p = & a;
```

The value of + +(* p) ?

(a) 24

(b) 25

(c) 26

(d) 31

10. The physical device for the stream stderr is

(a) Keyboard

(b) Printer

(c) Screen

(d) None of the above

11. If the function is initialised inside a function, it must be declared as

(a) static

(b) const

(c) auto

(d) extern

12. Mode 'a' allows to

(a) Read only

(b) Write only

(c) both

(d) append

13. Which of the following functions is more versatile for positioning the file pointer in a file?

   (a) rewind()

   (b) fseek()

   (c) ftell()

   (d) none

14.
```
main ( )
    {
    Printf("\n c to it that c survives ");
    Main( );
    }
```

   (a) FINITE

   (b) INFINITE

   (c) GARBAGE

   (d) NONE

15. If the array is initialised where it is declared, mentioning the dimension of the array is optional.

   (a) TRUE

   (b) FALSE

16. Which of the following expressions are the same

   (1) s[2][1]

   (2) *(s[2]+1)

   (3) *(*(s+2)+1)

   (a) all are same

   (b) 1 and 2 are same

   (c) 2 and 3 are same

   (d) 1 and 3 are same

17. If the fun c is a function needing three arguments a1,a2,a3 then fun c can be invoked by

(a) fun c(a1,a2,a3)

(b) (*fun c)(a1,a2,a3)

(c) *fun c(a1,a2,a3)

(d) All

18. A pointer is of

(a) Integer datatype

(b) Character datatype

(c) Unsigned integer data type

(d) None of the above

19. Which of the following statements will not add 1 to a variable?

(a) a++

(b) a+= 1

(c) a= a+1

(d) *p=*p+1;

(e) *p++

20. Which of the following defines and initialises a pointer to the address of x?

(a) int *ptr = *x;

(b) int * ptr = ^x;

(c) int * ptr = 2x;

(d) int 2 ptr = *x;

21. What is the output of the following program?

```
main( )
    {
        int n[25] ;
        n[0] = 100 ;
        n[24] = 200 ;
        printf("\n%d %d", *n, *(n+24) + *(n+0)) ;
        }
```

(a) 100, 300

(b) 100, 200

(c) 300, 100

(d) 200, 100

22.
```
int y[4] = { 6,7,8,9 } ;
int *ptr = y+2 ;
printf(" %d \n", ptr[1]) ;
/* ptr + 1 == ptr[1] */
```

What is printed when the sample code is executed?

(a) 6

(b) 7

(c) 8

(d) 9

23. **Which one of the following allocates, enough space to hold an array of 10 integers, that are initialised to 0?**

a. int *ptr = (int *) malloc (10, sizeof(int)) ;

b. int *ptr = (int *) calloc (10, sizeof(int)) ;

c. int *ptr = (int *) malloc (10*sizeof(int)) ;

d. int *ptr = (int *) alloc (10*sizeof(int)) ;

e. int *ptr = (int *) calloc (10*sizeof(int)) ;

(a) a

(b) b

(c) c

(d) d

(e) e

24. **What does the fgets function return when EOF is encountered?**

(a) 0

(b) 1

(c) -1

(d) NULL

25. & (address) operator can be used before:
   (a) an arithmetic expression
   (b) subscripted array elements
   (c) before unsubscripted array name
   (d) all of the above

26. If an array is declared as
   char z[10][12];
   what is referred to by z[5]?
   (a) error
   (b) 6th column of array
   (c) 5th row of array
   (d) 6th row of array

27. NULL is a macro defined in:
   (a) Stdio.h
   (b) Stdlib.h
   (c) tddef.h
   (d) Both a and c

28. What is the name of the * operator?
   (a) Pointer
   (b) Address of
   (c) Value at the address of
   (d) In directional operator

29.
```
#include<stdio.h>
#include<conio.h>
void main()
        {
        int k=35,z;
        k=func1(k=func1(k=func1(k)));
        printf("k=%d",k);
        }
func1(int k)
```

```
int k;
    {
    k++;
    return(k);
    }
```

(a) k=38

(b) k=35

(c) k=36

(d) Error

30. main()

```
    {
    int a = 30,b = 2,x;
    x = (( a != 10) && ( b = 50));
    printf(" x = %d", x );
    }
```

(a) x = 1

(b) x = 0

(c) x = 2

(d) None of the above

31. main()

```
    {
    int i = -4,j,num = 10;
    j = i % -3;
    j = (j ? 0 : num *num);
    printf("j = %d",j);
    }
```

(a) j = 1

(b) j = 0

(c) j = -1

(d) None of the above

32. main()

```
{
int i=0;
for( ;i;)
printf("\n i++");
}
```

(a) 0

(b) 1

(c) No output

(d) None of the above

33. main( )

```
{
int i = 1,j = 1;
for( ; j ; printf("%d %d\n" ,i , j ))
        j = i++ <= 5;
}
```

(a) 21 31 41 51 61 70.

(b) 1 2 3 4 5

(c) Error

(d) None of the above

34. for(i=0;i=5;i++) ;

(a) is loop forever

(b) Syntax error

(c) Loop will execute single time

(d) Loop will never execute

35. Which of the following not a unconditional branch statement?

(a) Return

(b) goto

(c) break

(d) All of the above are unconditional branch statements

36. Standard Template Library (STL) is created by?

(a) Alexander Stepanov

(b) Bjarne Stroustrup

(c) Denis Retche

(d) Lady Simula

37.
```
#include<stdio.h>
main()
    {
    char j=1;
    while(j<=225)
        {
        printf("%d\n",j);
        j=j+1;
        }
    }
```

(a) Error

(b) Print no. 1 to 255

(c) Abnormal termination

(d) Default values

38.
```
#include<stdio.h>
main()
    {
    int j=1;
    while(j<=255);
    {
    printf("%c %d\n",j,i);
    j++;
    }
```

(a) Abnormal termination

(b) Print no. with corresponding character

(c) Error

(d) Infinite loop

39.
```
#include<stdio.h>
main()
    {
    int i=1;
    for(;i++;)
        printf("%d",i);
    }
```
(a) 1

(b) 2 3...32767...-32768 -32767...-1 0

(c) 2

(d) Error

40.
```
#include<stdio.h>
main()
    {
    int x=3,y,z;
    z=y=x;
    z*=y/=x;
    printf("x=%d y=%d z=%d",x,y,z);
    }
```
(a) X=1 y=3 z=3

(b) X=3y=1z=3

(c) Error

(d) X=3 y=3 z=3

41. #include<stdio.h>

```
main()
    {
    int x=1,y=5;
    y*=x;
    printf("x=%d y=%d",x,y);
    }
```

(a) Garbage value

(b) X=1 y=1

(c) Error

(d) X=1 y=5

42. #include<stdio.h>

```
main()
    {
    int x,y,z;
    x=y=z=1;
    z=++x &&++y||++z;
    printf(x=%d y=%d z=%d\n",x,y,z);
    }
```

(a) x=1 y=1 z=1

(b) x=2 y=2 z=2

(c) x=2 y=2 z=1

(d) Error

43.
```
#include<stdio.h>
main()
    {
    int i=2,j=3,k,l;
    float a,b;
    k=i/j*j;
    l=j/i*i;
    a=i/j*j;
    b=j/i*i;
    printf("%d %d %f %f",k,l,a,b);
    }
```

(a) 0 0 0.000000 0.000000

(b) 0 2 0.000000 0.000000

(c) 0 2 0.000000 2.000000

(d) 1 1 0.000000 2.000000

44. A C variable cannot start with

(a) An alphabet

(b) A number

(c) A special symbol other than underscore

(d) Both (2) and (3) above

45.
```
#define DEF
main()
    {
    int i=2;
    #ifdef DEF
        printf("square of i=%d",i*i);
    #else
        printf("i=%d",i);
    #endif
    }
```

(a) Square of i=2

(b) I=2

(c) Square of i=4

(d) Error

46.
```
#define CUBE(X)(X*X*X)
main()
    {
    int a,b=3;
    a=CUBE(++b)/++b;
    printf("a=%d b=%d",a,b);
    }
```

(a) A=8 b=4

(b) A=9 b=4

(c) A=8 b=6

(d) A=49 b=7

47.
```
#define COND(a) if(a>=65 && a<=90)
main()
    {
    char ch='R';
    COND(ch)
        printf("Upper case");
    else
        printf("Lower case");
    }
```

(a) Error

(b) Uppercase

(c) Lowercase

(d) Abnormal termination

48. #define and &&

```
        #define OR ||
        #define LG <=
        #defin >=
main()
        {
        char ch='d';
        if((ch GE 65 AND ch LE 90) OR (ch AND GE 97 and LE 122))
            printf("Alphabet");
        else
            printf("not an alphabet");
        }
```

(a) Error

(b) Alphabet

(c) Abnormal Termination

(d) Not an alphabet

49. What is a pre-prossor directive?

(a) a message from compiler to a programmer

(b) a message from compiler to a linker

(c) a message from programmer to a pre-processor

(d) a message from programmer to the micro-processor

50. In a program the statement:

#include "filename"

is replaced by the contents of the file "filename"

(a) Before compilation

(b) After compilation

(c) During compilation

(d) None of the above

Answer Table

1	b	11	a	21	a	31	b	41	d
2	b	12	d	22	d	32	c	42	c
3	d	13	b	23	c	33	a	43	c
4	c	14	b	24	d	34	a	44	c
5	a	15	a	25	b	35	d	45	c
6	d	16	a	26	d	36	a	46	d
7	a	17	a,b	27	d	37	c	47	b
8	a	18	d	28	d	38	d	48	b
9	c	19	e	29	a	39	b	49	c
10	c	20	c	30	a	40	b	50	a

Objective Test-3

1.
```
#include<stdio.h>
#include<conio.h>
void main()
    {
    int z=4;
    printf("%d",printf("%d  %d",z,z));
    }
```
(a) 4 4 4

(b) Error

(c) 4 4 2

(d) 4 4 3

2.
```
#include<stdio.h>
#include<conio.h>
void main()
    {
    int i=10;
    clrscr();
    &i=7200;
printf("%d  %u",i,&i);
    getch();
    }
```
(a) 10 Garbage value

(b) 10 7200

(c) Error

(d) None of the above

3. #include"stdio.h"

```
main()
    {
    printf("%d%d",sizeof(NULL),sizeof(""));
    }
```

(a) 00

(b) 01

(c) 21

(d) 22

4. #include

```
#define a 10
main()
    {
    #define a 50
    printf("%d",a);
    }
```

(a) 50

(b) 10

(c) 100

(d) None

5. #include<stdio.h>

```
void main()
    {
    int a[]={10,20,30,40,50};
    int j;
    for(j=0;j<5;j++)
        {
        printf("\n%d",*a);
        a++;
        }
    getch():
    }
```

(a) Error

(b) 10 20 30 40 50

(c) 10 11 12 13 14

(d) Garbage value

6.
```
main()
{
Printf("Hello\b\b\b\b\b");
Printf("Hi!\b\b\bBye");
}
```

(a) YeloB

(b) Byelo

(c) Boyelo

(d) ByeHello

7.
```
#include<stdio.h>
main()
{
char s[]="Rendezvous !";
printf("\n%d",*(s+strlen(s));
}
```

(a) 10

(b) 11

(c) error

(d) 0

8. Find out errors if any:

```
#include"stdio.h"
main()
{
FILE *fp;
openfile("Myfile.txt",fp);
if(fp==NULL)
printf("unable to open file...");
}
```

(a) Line 1

(b) Line 5

(c) Line 6

(d) No errors

9. Complexity of merge sort is:-

(a) O(log n)

(b) O(n log n)

(c) $O(n^2)$

(d) $O(n^2 \log n)$

10. Complete graph with n nodes have _______ edges:-

(a) n/2

(b) (n-1)/2

(c) n(n-1)/2

(d) n(n+1)/2

11. What will be the output of the program?

```
main()
    {
    int a[5]={1,2,3,4,5};
    int *ptr;
    ptr=a;
    printf("%d",*ptr):
    ptr+=10;
    printf("%d",*ptr):
    }
```

(a) 1,5

(b) 1,0

(c) 1,Garbage value

(d) 1,15

12. main()

```
{
int arr[]={10,20,15,11,43};
int * i ,*j;
i=&arr[l];
j=&arr[5];
printf("%d%d",j-i,*j-*i);
}
```

(a) difference between 5th and 1st location of the array

(b) error

(c) 20 30

(d) none of the above

13. Find the output for the following C program

```
i=20,k=0;
for(j=1;j
  {
  k+=j<10?4:3;
  }
printf("%d", k);
```

(a) 1

(b) 2

(c) 3

(d) 4

14. which of the following statements are correct about the code given below:

```
main(int ac, char *av[])
  {
  }
```

(a) ac contains count of arg supplied at command line.

(b) av[] contains addresses of arg supplied at command line.

(c) in place of ac and av, argc and argv should be used.

(d) ac contains address of an integer whose value is equal to the count of arg supplied at command line.

15. fseek(fp,-1,SEEK_CUR), will move the pointer to the:
   (a) End of the file.
   (b) Will remain at same position of the pointer.
   (c) start of the file
   (d) error
   (e) none of the above

16. Which of the following statements is true:
   (a) %e read the floating point num
   (b) %g read the floating point num
   (c) %i read the hexadecimal num
   (d) none of the above

17. Which of the following functions may not be used to read from a text file "a.txt"?
   (a) getc
   (b) getchar
   (c) fgets
   (d) fscanf

18. If an array is declared as

```
char z[10][12];
```

what is referred to by z[5] ?
   (a) error
   (b) 6th column of array
   (c) 5th row of array
   (d) 6th row of array

19.

```
#define DIM( array, type) sizeof(array)/sizeof(type)
main()
{
int arr[10];
printf("The dimension of the array is %d", DIM(arr, int));
}
```

   (a) 7
   (b) 8

(c) 9

(d) 10

20.
```
main()
{
extern i;
printf("%d\n",i);
    {
    int i=20;
    printf("%d\n",i);
    }
}
```

(a) Linker Error

(b) RunTime Error

(c) Compilation Error

(d) Syntax Error

21.
```
main()
{
int a= 0;int b = 20;char x =1;char y =10;
if(a,b,x,y)
printf("hello");
}
```

(a) hello

(b) Syntax Error

(c) Infinite Loop

(d) None of the above

22.
```
main()
{
int i = -4,j,num = 10;
j = i % -3;
j = (j ? 0 : num *num);
printf("j = %d",j);
}
```

(a) j = 1

(b) j = 0

(c) j = -1

(d) None of the above

23.
```
main()
{
int i=_l_abc(10);
printf("%d\n",--i);
}
int _l_abc(int i)
{
return(i++);
}
```

(a) 4

(b) 7

(c) 9

(d) 3

24. double fabs (double x)

(a) Compute absolute value of x.

(b) Breaks down x into mantissa and exponent of no.

(c) Compute cosine of angle in radians

(d) Compute arc sine of x.

25.
```
#include
main()
{
FILE *ptr;
char i;
ptr=fopen("zzz.c","r");
while((i=fgetch(ptr))!=EOF)
	printf("%c",i);
}
```

(a) Error
(b) Infinite Loop
(c) zzz
(d) Compilation Error

26. 1. A structure combines
(a) Dissimilar data types
(b) Similar data types
(c) Only int and float
(d) Only char and int

27. Structure is always arranged in contiguous memory location
(a) True
(b) False

28. Which is true for the following statement?
A structure declaration that s not followed by a list of variables
(a) Reserves no storage
(b) Described as a template
(c) Definition of instances of structure
(d) All of the above

29. FILE is
(a) Variable
(b) Pre-processor declarative
(c) Define data type
(d) Standard data type

30. While opening in append mode if file does not exist then
(a) A new file is created
(b) error occurs
(c) file open in write mode
(d) program terminates abruptly

31. getw and putw are ________ oriented function.
   (a) word
   (b) integer
   (c) text
   (d) byte
32. fscanf returns
   (a) the index position
   (b) number of items successfully read
   (c) 1 if item is read
   (d) 0 if error occurs
33. feof function is used to
   (a) go to the end of file
   (b) test for end of file condition
   (c) check for errors
   (d) terminate the program
34. In the code : fseek(fin,2,1)
   Here the value 1 is used to go to the
   (a) Current position
   (b) Beginning of file
   (c) End of file
   (d) Go to the 1st position of file
35. C programming is
   (a) Procedural and functional oriented
   (b) procedural, imperative computer programming language
   (c) procedural and declarative language
   (d) Object oriented language

36. Which of the following file opening modes would overwrite the file being opened, if the file already exits on the disk?

    (a) "w"

    (b) "wb"

    (c) "wb+"

    (d) "rb+"

    (e) "ab+"

37. Which of the following functions are ideally suited for reading the contents of a file record by record?

    (a) getc()

    (b) gets()

    (c) fread()

    (d) fgets()

38. The requirement is that the program should receive a key from the keyboard. However, the key that is hit should not appear on the screen. Which of the following functions would you use?

    (a) getch()

    (b) getche()

    (c) getchar()

    (d) fgetchar()

39. The FILE structure is defined in which of the following files:

    (a) stdlib.h

    (b) stdio.h

    (c) io.h

    (d) conio.h

40. If a file contains a line "I am a boy\r\n" then on reading this line into the array str[] using fgets() what would str[] contain?

    (a) I am a boy\r\n\0

    (b) 2: I am a boy\r\0

    (c) 3: I am a boy\n\0

    (d) 4: I am a boy

41. Which of the following language is predecessor to C programming language?
   (a) A
   (b) B
   (c) C++
   (d) PASCAL

42 What does the following statement mean?

Int (*a)[4]

   (a) 'a' is a pointer to an array of 4 integers
   (b) 'a' is an array of pointers to integer
   (c) 'a' is a pointer to function returning an integer
   (d) none of the above

43. Find the output of the following program

```
int *p,*q;
p=(int *)1000;
q=(int *)2000;
printf("%d",(q-p));
```

   (a) 234
   (b) 500
   (c) 300
   (d) 400

44.

```
void main()
    {
    char *s="\12345s\n";
    printf("%d",sizeof(s));
     }
```

   (a) 3
   (b) 4
   (c) 6
   (d) 7

45.
```
void main()
{
int i=7;
printf("%d",i++*i++);
}
```
(a) 54
(b) 56
(c) 58
(d) 59

46.
```
main()
{
 static i=3;
printf("%d",i--);
return i>0 ? main():0;
}
```
(a) 319
(b) 320
(c) 321
(d) 323

47.
```
int x=2;
x=x<<2;
printf("%d ",x);
```
(a) 5
(b) 8
(c) 11
(d) 9

48. malloc function allocates memory at
(a) compilation time
(b) link
(c) load
(d) running

49. which is the 16-bit max signed int.

(a) 66337

(b) 66338

(c) 257

(d) 258

50. square(x) x*x

a=10 b=20

if called as printf("%d", square(a+b)); what will be the output

(a) 229

(b) 230

(c) 231

(d) 232

Answer Table

1	d	11	c	21	a	31	b	41	b
2	c	12	d	22	b	32	b	42	a
3	c	13	d	23	c	33	b	43	b
4	a	14	a,b	24	a	34	a	44	c
5	a	15	e	25	b	35	b	45	b
6	b	16	a,b	26	a	36	a,b,c	46	c
7	d	17	b	27	a	37	c	47	b
8	b	18	d	28	d	38	a	48	d
9	b	19	d	29	c	39	b	49	a
10	c	20	a	30	a	40	c	50	b

Appendices

Appendix-I: List of ASCII Symbols

0	NUL	35	#	70	F	105	i
1	SOH	36	$	71	G	106	j
2	STX	37	%	72	H	107	k
3	ETX	38	&	73	I	108	l
4	EOT	39	'	74	J	109	m
5	ENQ	40	(	75	K	110	n
6	ACK	41	)	76	L	111	o
7	BEL	42	*	77	M	112	p
8	BS	43	+	78	N	113	q
9	HT	44	,	79	O	114	r
10	LF	45	-	80	P	115	s
11	VT	46	.	81	Q	116	t
12	FF	47	/	82	R	117	u
13	CR	48	0	83	S	118	v
14	SO	49	1	84	T	119	w
15	SI	50	2	85	U	120	x
16	DLE	51	3	86	V	121	y
17	DC1	52	4	87	W	122	z
18	DC2	53	5	88	X	123	{
19	DC3	54	6	89	Y	124	|
20	DC4	55	7	90	Z	125	}
21	NAK	56	8	91	[	126	~
22	SYM	57	9	92	\	127	DEL
23	ETB	58	:	93	]		
24	CAN	59	;	94	^		
25	EM	60	<	95	_		
26	SUB	61	=	96	`		
27	ESC	62	>	97	a		
28	FS	63	?	98	b		
29	GS	64	@	99	c		
30	RS	65	A	100	d		
31	US	66	B	101	e		
32	SP	67	C	102	f		
33	!	68	D	103	g		
34	"	69	E	104	h		

Appendix-II: List of C Keywords and Operators

Keywords in C Language:

auto	break	case	char	const	continue	default
do	double	else	enum	extern	float	for
goto	if	int	long	register	return	short
signed typedef	sizeof union		static	struct		switch
unsigned	void	volatile	while			

Operators in C Language:

Operator	Meaning
+	Addition or Unary Plus
-	Subtraction or Unary Minus
*	Multiplication
/	Division
%	Modulus Operator (Remainder)
<	is less than
<=	is less than or equal to
>	is greater than
>=	is greater than or equal to
==	is equal to
!=	is not equal to
&&	Logical AND
||	Logical OR
!	Logical NOT
+=	Plus equal to
-=	Minus equal to
*=	Multiply equal to
/=	Divide equal to
%=	Modulus equal to
++	X++
- -	Y - -
?:	Ternary operator
&	Bitwise AND

|	Bitwise OR
^	Bitwise Exclusive
<<	Shift left
>>	Shift right
Sizeof	Sizeof

Operator Precedence:

Order	Category	Operator	Operation	Associativity
1	Highest precedence	( ) [ ] → :: .	Function call	L → R Left to Right
2	Unary	! ~ + - ++ - - & * Size of	Logical negation (NOT) Bitwise 1's complement Unary plus Unary minus Pre-or post-increment Pre-or post-decrement Address Indirection Size of operant in bytes	R → L Right to Left
3	Member Access	.* →*	De-reference De-reference	L → R
4	Multiplication	* / %	Multiply Divide Modulus	
5	Additive	+ -	Binary Plus Binary Minus	L → R
6	Shift	<< >>	Shift Left Shift Right	
7	Relational	< <= > >=	Less than Less than or equal to Greater than Greater than or equal to	L → R

8	Equality	== !=	Equal to Not Equal to	L ⟶ R
9	Bitwise AAND	&	Bitwise AND	L ⟶ R
10	Bitwise X OR	^	Bitwise XOR	L ⟶ R
11	Bitwise OR	|	Bitwise OR	L ⟶ R
12	Logical AND	&&	Logical AND	L ⟶ R
14	Conditional	? :	Ternary Operator	R ⟶ L
15	Assignment	= *= %= /= += -= &= ^= |= <<= >>=	Assignment Assign product Assign reminder Assign quotient Assign sum Assign difference Assign bitwise AND Assign bitwise XOR Assign bitwise OR Assign left shift Assign right shift	R ⟶ L

Appendix-III: List of Commonly used Functions from Standard C Library

Header File	Function	Declaration	Description
assert.h	assert	void assert(int expression);	The assert macro allows diagnostic information to be written to the standard error file. If expression evaluates to 0 (false), then the expression, source code filename, and line number are sent to the standard error, and then calls the abort function.
ctype.h	isalnum();	int isalnum(int character);	a letter (A to Z or a to z) or a digit (0 to 9)
	isalpha();	int isalpha(int character);	a letter (A to Z or a to z)
	iscntrl();	int iscntrl(int character);	any control character (0x00 to 0x1F or 0x7F)
	isdigit();	int isdigit(int character);	a digit (0 to 9)
	isgraph();	int isgraph(int character);	any printing character except for the space character (0x21 to 0x7E)
	islower();	int islower(int character);	a lowercase letter (a to z)
	isprint();	int isprint(int character);	any printing character (0x20 to 0x7E)
	isspace();	int isspace(int character);	a whitespace character (space, tab, carriage return, new line, vertical tab, or formfeed)
	isupper();	int isupper(int character);	an uppercase letter (A to Z)
	isxdigit();	int isxdigit(int character);	a hexadecimal digit (0 to 9, A to F, or a to f)
	tolower();	int tolower(int character);	If the character is an uppercase character (A to Z), then it is converted to lowercase (a to z)
	toupper();	int toupper(int character);	If the character is a lowercase character (a to z), then it is converted to uppercase (A to Z)

errno.h	EDOM	#define EDOM some_value	EDOM is an identifier macro declared with #define.
	ERANGE	#define ERANGE some_value	ERANGE is an identifier macro declared with #define.
	errno	int errno;	
float.h		sign value E exponent	The float header defines the minimum and maximum limits of floating-point number values
limits.h			The limits header defines the characteristics of variable types.
locale.h	Structure	struct lconv	The locale header is useful for setting location specific information.
	Macros	NULL	
		LC_ALL	Set everything
		LC_COLLATE	Affects strcoll and strxfrm functions
		LC_CTYPE	Affects all character functions
		LC_MONETARY	Affects the monetary information provided by localeconv function
		LC_NUMERIC	Affects decimal-point formatting and the information provided by localeconv function
		LC_TIME	Affects the strftime function localeconv(); struct lconv *localeconv(void); Sets the structure lconv to represent the current location settings. setlocale(); char *setlocale (int category, const char *locale); Sets or reads location dependent information.
math.h	acos();	double acos(double x);	Returns the arc cosine of x in radians.
	asin();	double asin(double x);	Returns the arc sine of x in radians.

	atan();	double atan(double x);	Returns the arc tangent of x in radians
	atan2();	double atan2(doubly y, double x);	Returns the arc tangent in radians of y/x based on the signs of both values to determine the correct quadrant.
	ceil();	double ceil(double x);	Returns the smallest integer value greater than or equal to x.
	cos();	double cos(double x);	Returns the cosine of a radian angle x.
	cosh();	double cosh(double x);	Returns the hyperbolic cosine of x.
	exp();	double exp(double x);	Returns the value of e raised to the xth power.
	fabs();	double fabs(double x);	Returns the absolute value of x (a negative value becomes positive, positive value is unchanged).
	floor();	double floor(double x);	Returns the largest integer value less than or equal to x.
	fmod();	double fmod(double x, double y);	Returns the remainder of x divided by y.
	frexp();	double frexp(double x, int *exponent);	The floating-point number x is broken up into a mantissa and exponent. The returned value is the mantissa and the integer pointed to by exponent is the exponent. The resultant value is x=mantissa * 2^exponent.
	ldexp();	double ldexp(double x, int exponent);	Returns x multiplied by 2 raised to the power of exponent. x*2^exponent
	log();	double log(double x);	Returns the natural logarithm (base-e logarithm) of x.
	log10();	double log10(double x);	Returns the common logarithm (base-10 logarithm) of x.
	modf();	double modf(double x, double *integer);	Breaks the floating-point number x into integer and fraction components.

			The returned value is the fraction component (part after the decimal), and sets integer to the integer component.
	pow();	double pow(double x, double y);	Returns x raised to the power of y.
	sin();	double sin(double x);	Returns the sine of a radian angle x.
	sinh();	double sinh(double x);	Returns the hyperbolic sine of x.
	sqrt();	double sqrt(double x);	Returns the square root of x.
	tan();	double tan(double x);	Returns the tangent of a radian angle x.
	tanh();	double tanh(double x);	Returns the hyperbolic tangent of x
setjmp.h	setjmp();	int setjmp(jmp_buf environment);	Saves the environment into the variable environment. If a non-zero value is returned, then this indicates that the point in the sourcecode was reached by a longjmp. Otherwise zero is returned indicating the environment has been saved.
	longjmp();	void longjmp(jmp_buf environment, int value);	Causes the environment to be restored from a setjmp call where the environment variable had been saved
signal.h	Macros: SIG_DFL		Default handler
	SIG_ERR		Represents a signal error.
	SIG_IGN		Signal ignore.
	SIGABRT		Abnormal termination (generated by the abort function).
	SIGFPE		Floating-point error (error caused by division by zero, invalid operation, etc.).
	SIGILL		Illegal operation (instruction).
	SIGINT		Interactive attention signal (such as ctrl-C).

	SIGSEGV		Invalid access to storage (segment violation, memory violation).
	SIGTERM		Termination request.
	signal();	void (*signal(int sig, void (*func)(int)))(int);	Controls how a signal is handled. sig represents the signal number compatible with the SIG macros. func is the function to be called when the signal occurs.
	raise();	int raise(int sig);	Causes signal sig to be generated. The sig argument is compatible with the SIG macros.
stdarg.h	va_start();	void va_start(va_list ap, last_arg);	Initialises ap for use with the va_arg and va_end macros. last_arg is the last known fixed argument being passed to the function
	va_arg();	type va_arg(va_list ap, type);	Expands to the next argument in the paramater list of the function with type type.
	va_end();	void va_end(va_list ap);	Allows a function with variable arguments which used the va_start macro to return.
stddef.h	offsetof();	offsetof(type, member-designator)	This results in a constant integer of type size_t which is the offset in bytes of a structure member from the beginning of the structure.
stdio.h	_IOFBF	_IOFBF, _IOLBF, and _IONBF are used in the setvbuf function.	
	_IOLBF		
	_IONBF		
	BUFSIZ	BUFSIZ is an integer which represents the size of the buffer used by the setbuf function.	
	EOF	EOF is a negative integer which indicates an end-of-file has been reached.	
	FOPEN_MAX	FOPEN_MAX is an integer which represents the maximum number of files that the system can guarantee that can be opened simultaneously.	

FILENAME_ MAX	FILENAME_MAX is an integer which represents the longest length of a char array suitable for holding the longest possible filename.	
L_tmpnam	L_tmpnam is an integer which represents the longest length of a char array suitable for holding the longest possible temporary filename created by the tmpnam function.	
SEEK_CUR	SEEK_CUR, SEEK_END, and SEEK_SET are used in the fseek function.	
SEEK_END		
SEEK_SET		
TMP_MAX	TMP_MAX is the maximum number of unique filenames that the function tmpnam can generate.	
Stderr Stdin Stdout	stderr, stdin, and stdout are pointers to FILE types which correspond to the standard error, standard input, and standard output streams.	
clearerr();	void clearerr(FILE *stream);	Clears the end-of-file and error indicators for the given stream.
fclose();	int fclose(FILE *stream);	Closes the stream. All buffers are flushed.
feof();	int feof(FILE *stream);	Tests the end-of-file indicator for the given stream.
ferror();	int ferror(FILE *stream);	Tests the error indicator for the given stream.
fflush();	int fflush(FILE *stream);	Flushes the output buffer of a stream.
fgetpos();	int fgetpos(FILE *stream, fpos_t *pos);	Gets the current file position of the stream and writes it to pos.
fopen();	FILE *fopen(const char *filename, const char *mode);	Opens the filename pointed to by filename.
fread();	size_t fread(void *ptr, size_t size, size_t nmemb, FILE *stream);	Reads data from the given stream into the array pointed to by ptr.
freopen();	FILE *freopen(const char *filename, const char *mode, FILE *stream);	Associates a new filename with the given open stream.
fseek();	int fseek(FILE *stream, long int offset, int whence);	Sets the file position of the stream to the given offset.
fsetpos();	int fsetpos(FILE *stream, const fpos_t *pos);	Sets the file position of the given stream to the given position.

ftell();	long int ftell(FILE *stream);	Returns the current file position of the given stream.
fwrite();	size_t fwrite(const void *ptr, size_t size, size_t nmemb, FILE *stream);	Writes data from the array pointed to by ptr to the given stream.
remove();	int remove(const char Deletes *filename);	the given filename so that it is no longer accessible
rename();	int rename(const char *old_filename, const char to *new_filename);	Causes the filename referred by old_filename to be changed to new_filename.
rewind();	void rewind(FILE *stream);	Sets the file position to the beginning of the file of the given stream.
setbuf();	void setbuf(FILE *stream, char *buffer);	Defines how a stream should be buffered.
setvbuf();	int setvbuf(FILE *stream, char *buffer, int mode, size_t size);	Defines how a stream should be buffered
tmpfile();	FILE *tmpfile(void);	Creates a temporary file in binary update mode (wb+). The tempfile is removed when the program terminates or the stream is closed.
tmpnam();	char *tmpnam(char *str);	Generates and returns a valid temporary filename which does not exist.
fprintf();	int fprintf(FILE *stream, const char *format, ...);	Sends formatted output to a stream
fscanf();	int fscanf(FILE *stream, const char *format, ...);	Reads formatted input from a stream
printf();	int printf(const char *format, ...);	Sends formatted output to stdout
scanf();	int scanf(const char *format, ...);	Reads formatted input from stdin
sprintf();	int sprintf(char *str, const char *format, ...);	Sends formatted output to a string
sscanf();	int sscanf(const char *str, const char *format, ...);	Reads formatted input from a string
vfprintf();	int vfprintf(FILE *stream, const char *format, va_list arg);	Sends formatted output to a stream using an argument list

	vprintf();	int vprintf(const char *format, va_list arg);;	Sends formatted output to stdout using an argument list
	vsprintf();	int vsprintf(char *str, const char *format, va_list arg)	sends formatted output to a string using an argument list
	fgetc();	int fgetc(FILE *stream);	Gets the next character (an unsigned char) from the specified stream and advances the position indicator for the stream.
	fgets();	char *fgets(char *str, int n, FILE *stream);	Reads a line from the specified stream and stores it into the string pointed to by str.
	fputc();	int fputc(int char, FILE *stream);	Writes a character (an unsigned char) specified by the argument char to the specified stream and advances the position indicator for the stream.
	fputs();	int fputs(const char *str, FILE *stream);	Writes a string to the specified stream up to but not including the null character.
	getc();	int getc(FILE *stream);	Gets the next character (an unsigned char) from the specified stream and advances the position indicator for the stream.
	getchar();	int getchar(void);	Gets a character (an unsigned char) from stdin.
	gets();	char *gets(char *str);	Reads a line from stdin and stores it into the string pointed to by str.
	putc();	int putc(int char, FILE *stream);	Writes a character (an unsigned char) specified by the argument char to the specified stream and advances the position indicator for the stream.
	putchar();	int putchar(int char);	Writes a character (an unsigned char) specified by the argument char to stdout.

	puts();	int puts(const char *str);	Writes a string to stdout up to but not including the null character.
	ungetc();	int ungetc(int char, FILE *stream);	Pushes the character char (an unsigned char) onto the specified stream so, that this is the next character read.
	perror();	void perror(const char *str);	Prints a descriptive error message to stderr.
stdlib.h	abort();	void abort(void);	Causes an abnormal program termination.
	abs();	int abs(int x);	Returns the absolute value of x.
	atexit();	int atexit(void (*func)(void));	Causes the specified function to be called when the program terminates normally.
	atof();	double atof(const char *str);	The string pointed to by the argument str is converted to a floating-point number (type double).
	atoi();	int atoi(const char *str);	The string pointed to by the argument str is converted to an integer (type int).
	atol();	long int atol(const char *str);	The string pointed to by the argument str is converted to a long integer
	bsearch();	void *bsearch(const void *key, const void *base, size_t nitems, size_t size, int (*compar)(const void *, const void *));	Performs a binary search.
	calloc();	void *calloc(size_t nitems, size_t size);	Allocates the requested memory and returns a pointer to it.
	div();	div_t div(int numer, int denom);	Divides numer (numerator) by denom (denominator).
	free();	void free(void *ptr);	Deallocates the memory previously allocated by a call to calloc, malloc, or realloc.
	exit();	void exit(int status);	Causes the program to terminate normally.

getenv();	char *getenv(const char *name);	Searches for the environment string pointed to by name and returns the associated value to the string.
labs();	long int labs(long int x);	Returns the absolute value of x.
ldiv();	ldiv_t ldiv(long int numer, long int denom);	Divides numer (numerator) by denom (denominator).
malloc();	void *malloc(size_t size);	Allocates the requested memory and returns a pointer to it.
mblen();	int mblen(const char *str, size_t n);	Returns the length of a multibyte character pointed to by the argument str.
mbstowcs()	size_t mbstowcs (schar_t *pwcs, const char *str, size_t n);	Converts the string of multibyte characters pointed to by the argument str to the array pointed to by pwcs.
mbtowc();	int mbtowc(whcar_t *pwc, const char *str, size_t n);	Examines the multibyte character pointed to by the argument str.
qsort();	void qsort(void *base, size_t nitems, size_t size, int (*compar)(const void *, const void*));	Sorts an array.
rand();	int rand(void);	Returns a pseudo-random number in the range of 0 to RAND_MAX.
realloc();	void *realloc(void *ptr, size_t size);	Attempts to resize the memory block pointed to by ptr that was previously allocated with a call to malloc or calloc.
srand();	void srand(unsigned int seed);	This function seeds the random number generator used by the function rand.
strtod();	double strtod(const char *str, char **endptr);	The string pointed to by the argument str is converted to a floating-point number
strtol();	long int strtol(const char *str, char **endptr, int base);	The string pointed to by the argument str is converted to a long integer (type long int).

	strtoul();	unsigned long int strtoul (const char *str, char **endptr, int base);	The string pointed to by the argument str is converted to an unsigned long integer (type unsigned long int).
	system();	int system(const char *string);	The command specified by string is passed to the host environment to be executed by the command processor.
	wcstombs();	size_t wcstombs(char *str, const wchar_t *pwcs, size_t n);	Converts the codes stored in the array pwcs to multibyte characters and stores them in the string str.
	wctomb();	int wctomb(char *str, wchar_t wchar);	Examines the code which corresponds to a multibyte character given by the argument wchar.
string.h	memchr();	void *memchr(const void *str, int c, size_t n);	Searches for the first occurrence of the character c (an unsigned char) in the first n bytes of the string pointed to by the argument str.
	memcmp();	int memcmp(const void *str1, const void *str2, size_t n);	Compares the first n bytes of str1 and str2. Does not stop comparing even after the null character (it always checks n characters).
	memcpy();	void *memcpy(void *str1, const void *str2, size_t n);	Copies n characters from str2 to str1. If str1 and str2 overlap the behaviour is undefined.
	memmove();	void *memmove(void *str1, const void *str2, size_t n);	Copies n characters from str2 to str1.
	memset();	void *memset(void *str, int c, size_t n);	Copies the character c (an unsigned char) to the first n characters of the string pointed to by the argument str.
	strcat();	char *strcat(char *str1, const char *str2);	Appends the string pointed to by str2 to the end of the string pointed to by str1.
	strncat();	char *strncat(char *str1, const char *str2, size_t n);	Appends the string pointed to by str2 to the end of the string pointed to by str1 up to n characters long.

	strchr();	char *strchr(const char *str, int c);	Searches for the first occurrence of the character c (an unsigned char) in the string pointed to by the argument str.
	strcmp();	int strcmp(const char *str1, const char *str2);	Compares the string pointed to by str1 to the string pointed to by str2.
	strncmp();	int strncmp(const char *str1, const char *str2, size_t n);	Compares at most the first n bytes of str1 and str2. Stops comparing after the null character.
	strcoll();	int strcoll(const char *str1, const char *str2);	Compares string str1 to str2. The result is dependent on the LC_COLLATE setting of the location.
	strcpy();	char *strcpy(char *str1, const char *str2);	Copies the string pointed to by str2 to str1.
	strncpy();	char *strncpy(char *str1, const char *str2, size_t n);	Copies up to n characters from the string pointed to by str2 to str1.
	strcspn();	size_t strcspn(const char *str1, const char *str2);	Finds the first sequence of characters in the string str1 that does not contain any character specified in str2.
	strlen();	size_t strlen(const char *str);	Computes the length of the string str up to but not including the terminating null character.
	strpbrk();	char *strpbrk(const char *str1, const char *str2);	Finds the first character in the string str1 that matches any character specified in str2.
	strrchr();	char *strrchr(const char *str, int c);	Searches for the last occurrence of the character c (an unsigned char) in the string pointed to by the argument str. The terminating null character is considered to be part of the string.
	strspn();	size_t strspn(const char *str1, const char *str2);	Finds the first sequence of characters in the string str1 that contains any character specified in str2.

	strstr();	char *strstr(const char *str1, const char *str2);	Finds the first occurrence of the entire string str2 (not including the terminating null character) which appears in the string str1.
	strtok();	char *strtok(char *str1, const char *str2);	Breaks string str1 into a series of tokens. If str1 and str2 are not null, then the following search sequence begins.
	strxfrm();	size_t strxfrm(char *str1, const char *str2, size_t n);	Transforms the string str2 and places the result into str1.
	strerror();	char *strerror(int errnum);	Searches an internal array for the error number errnum and returns a pointer to an error message string.
time.h	asctime();	char *asctime(const struct tm *timeptr);	Returns a pointer to a string which represents the day and time of the structure timeptr.
	clock();	clock_t clock(void);	Returns the processor clock time used since the beginning of an implementation-defined era (normally the beginning of the program).
	ctime();	char *ctime(const time _t *timer);	Returns a string representing the localtime based on the argument timer.
	difftime();	double difftime(time_t time1, time_t time2);	Calculates the difference of seconds between time1 and time2 (time1-time2). Returns the number of seconds.
	gmtime();	struct tm *gmtime (const time_t *timer);	The value of timer is broken up into the structure tm and expressed in Coordinated Universal Time (UTC) also known as Greenwich Mean Time (GMT).
	localtime();	struct tm *localtime (const time_t *timer);	The value of timer is broken up into the structure tm and expressed in the local time zone.

	mktime();	time_t mktime (struct tm *timeptr);	Converts the structure pointed to by timeptr into a time_t value according to the local time zone.
	strftime();	size_t strftime(char *str, size_t maxsize, const char *format, const struct tm *timeptr);	Formats the time represented in the structure timeptr according to the formatting rules defined in format and stored into str. No more than maxsize characters are stored into str (including the terminating null character).
	time();	time_t time(time_t *timer);	Calculates the current calendar time and encodes it into time_t format.

END